Trust-Based Selling

Also by Kerry Johnson

New Mindset, New Results

*Why Smart People Make Dumb Mistakes
With Their Money*

Willpower

Mastering Self-Confidence with NLP

Phone Sales

Sales Magic

How to Read Your Client's Mind

Peak Performance

Trust-Based Selling

ADVANCED TECHNIQUES ON GAINING RAPPORT AND TRUST

Kerry Johnson, MBA, Ph.D.

MEDIA

Published 2020 by Gildan Media LLC
aka G&D Media
www.GandDmedia.com

FIRST EDITION 2020

Front Cover design by David Rheinhardt of Pyrographx

Interior design by Meghan Day Healey of Story Horse, LLC

Library of Congress Cataloging-in-Publication Data is available upon request

ISBN: 978-1-7225-0184-6

10   9   8   7   6   5   4   3   2   1

Contents

Introduction

Why is it that some people, with just a few gestures or words, can communicate mountains of knowledge and information and evoke emotion from their listeners to such an extent that the listeners become committed and dedicated to what the speaker says?

In this book, you will learn about subliminal seduction in advertising research and how you can apply it in selling or interpersonal communication. You'll learn how the unconscious mind works and how you can directly appeal and present information to the unconscious. You will learn how to effectively bypass consciousness in communicating ideas. You'll also learn some of the simplest and yet most fundamental ways of how to be an effective communicator with everyone.

In the first chapter, you'll learn about a type of people called *visuals*. You'll learn how to identify them and understand what they're like. You'll also learn what goes through heads of visuals, and some very effective techniques for getting them to do what you want them to do.

Chapter 2 will cover another group, called *auditories*. You'll learn how to identify them and their characteristics, how they think, and how to talk to them. You'll find out how to deal with them and present information as well as how to close them.

In chapter 3, we will deal with *kinesthetics*—learning how they think, what they're like, how they behave, and also how to persuade, sell, and communicate with them. In this way you'll be able to get them to act and react in the way that you'd like.

Furthermore, you'll learn how to get more trust and more rapport faster than you ever thought possible with techniques called *matching* and *mirroring*. I'll share with you some specific persuasion techniques on the telephone. You'll learn how to change someone's attitude just by using subliminal messages.

Other techniques will explore how to anchor people's emotions, how to get people to say yes, and psychological sliding. You'll also learn about *instant replay*, or how to get your prospect's own unique decision or buying strategy. You'll gain useful information on understanding exactly what your prospect wants within the first few minutes. So guess what? You can give it to them.

You'll learn how to use better techniques for overcoming objections. You'll gain information on how to use metaphors and stories in a way that the prospect wants to hear them. Perhaps, most importantly, I'll show you how to wrap all these techniques together so you can make more money by communicating with people the way they want to be communicated with instead of the way you want to communicate with them.

When you finish this book, I hope you'll agree that it offers some of the most sophisticated, useful, and unusual selling and persuasion techniques you have ever seen. Be prepared to sell more in the next few days and weeks than you have previously sold in your whole life.

The best ways to keep from quickly forgetting these ideas are, number one, practice at least one technique each day in a real-life situation, and number two, teach these techniques to two other people. This will solidify these ideas in your mind and help you find more applications for the concepts.

One

Visuals: How to Get People to See Things

This research came about as a result of a lot of studies in my last couple of years at the University of California, San Diego on subliminal seduction in advertising. Have you ever seen a subliminal message in advertising? Gilbey's Gin did a study in which they found out they could sell a whole lot more gin if they could entrance or entrap you. Gilbey's investigated some of the most interesting and unique studies for subliminally influencing your mind, getting you to pay more attention to the subliminal messages that are inside ad photos. In one ad, you see Gilbey's Gin over here, but there are interesting little letters in the ice cubes. There's an **S** in the one at the top. You'll see an **E** in the middle. Guess what the letter in the bottom ice cube letter is.

Every time Gilbey's runs this ad, they pay $50,000 to $70,000 to magazines like *Playboy, Playgirl, Time, Newsweek.* You know what their return on investment is from using this thing? Five million to seven million dollars every time. You've been sold things you haven't even wanted for years and years, and they know in technology how to give it to you at the right time at the right place.

Have you been to Las Vegas? You've probably seen the lights in Las Vegas go fairly slowly, at hypnotic levels, trying to entrance you into putting more money into their biggest revenue-producers, which are slot machines. You will never play a slot machine by itself in a casino. You only play them in groups of four, five, six together around you. Why? Because Las Vegas wants you to hear the money down the chutes on the other slot machines that you're not playing. "This thing's going to hit any second now. How come all the rest of them are hitting and mine isn't?" Aladdin's and Caesar's Palace casinos are now etching in nude figures into the glass of those slot machines. Keeps you there a whole lot longer, doesn't it?

Kmart is doing almost the same thing. They've made their lights go down to fairly hypnotic levels. They made blue lights flash around to captivate small minds. Kmart is also doing something interesting with Muzak. We've known in industrial psychology that Muzak, if used the right way, will increase worker performance and decrease worker tension; otherwise the Muzak Corporation would not be so enormously profitable. Kmart is now putting unconscious soundtrack messages below that Muzak, which repeat over and over again during all store hours: "Please, don't steal. We want you to buy, buy, buy." Their consumption has increased by 9 percent more than expectations in the same time frame. What are some of the first words children learn these days? "Attention, K-Mart shoppers."

Have you ever been with a prospect face-to-face, belly button to belly button, toenail to toenail but felt you weren't quite getting through to that guy? Or have you felt that the prospect didn't quite see, hear, and feel the same way that you did about your product?

One more question: is your closing rate at 100 percent?

Here are three benefits I hope you will get from this book.

1. You're going to find out more about your prospects in five minutes than you previously could in two weeks.

2. You're going to find out how to get more trust from your prospect faster than you ever thought possible.

3. Probably the most important part: you're going to be able to double your business this year by using these techniques, because you're going to learn how to understand what your prospect is thinking at the time they think it.

Important to you so far? I hope so, because you're going to get a lot from this book. Actually a lot of the research came from observing top sellers. But here's the secret: they don't know why they're doing so much business. They have no idea why they're so successful. Have you heard these guys speak at sales conferences or conventions? You know that they say? "You have to have a positive mental attitude. You have to be a winner. You have to know what you want in life."

That doesn't tell you *how* they're selling. They tell you what they think they're doing, but they frankly don't know. They have what we call *unconscious competence*. One time I was talking to a high producer named John Savage. "John," I said, "this is the way you're selling. These are the tools you're using with your prospects."

"Kerry," he said, "you're one of the only psychologists I know in the country who has his feet firmly planted in midair."

John Savage once did $128,000 in commissions in a single month. His vice president of marketing called up and said, "John, $128,000 in January—what are you going to do in February?"

John said, "Not a damn thing."

I'd like you to write down answers to three questions.

1. Write down the first number between one and ten that you can think of.
2. Write down your favorite flower.
3. Write down the first word you think of when I say the word *table*.

   If you're a male, add this:
4. Write down your favorite color.

Chances are you said either three or seven for the numbers. Chances are you picked *rose* when I said *flower* and wrote *chair* when I said *table*. If you're male, you probably said that blue is your favorite color. You are so predictable.

Here are another couple of benefits I will show you. I'll show how you can observe, predict, and control—how you can observe people so well that you'll predict what they'll do in almost any situation. As a result, you'll be able to control yourself when you're with them; if you have to, you can even control their responses.

Our research shows that you don't understand your prospect's head map yet. You don't understand how your prospect thinks yet. This is unfortunate, because basically your prospects think in very unique and specific ways.

Your prospect's head is organized like this. It has Mark Twain Avenue, Comanche Boulevard, maybe 103rd Street. Your map is a little bit different. You have South Street up there, California Avenue, Century Boulevard. The problem is, if you don't understand what your prospect's map looks like, you're only communicating information. You're not communicating intent and meaning, which impart trust.

If you don't understand what your prospect's map look like, you're selling by accident. You happen to say the word at the right time, and they go for it. Have you ever sold by accident? They just said, "OK," and you had enough sense to stop talking. I think that's bright in itself.

One of my professors said, "Kerry, there are three states of reality: how you see it, how they see it, and how it really is." I told this once to a life-insurance underwriter in Des Moines, and he said, "Kerry, there's a fourth reality—how California people see it."

Here is a truth: if you can see John Smith through John Smith's eyes, you can sell John Smith what John Smith buys. I'm going to show you what John Smith's map looks like so that you can understand what John Smith buys and how you can sell it to him. You're going to understand how John Smith buys by listening to him very closely.

You may have heard that if you can get your prospects to see it, hear it, and feel it, they'll probably go for it. That is almost complete garbage. Your prospects don't do all three things at once. They *either* see things, hear things, or feel things that are organized in specific ways, but they can't understand all that information at one time. Your prospects are basically broken up into three groups. The first get more information from the things that they can see, the images that you portray and paint for them while you talk than from anything that you actually say. These are called *visuals*.

There's a second group, called *auditories*. These individuals can understand more from what they hear—the way they hear it, the delivery, the pace, the pitch, the tone—than from the content or from the logic with which you say it.

The third group is called *kinesthetics*. They buy because of gut feeling, sometimes called "trust," sometimes "gut response." Kinesthetics are easy to spot, because they will buy just because of the way they feel about you.

There are two ways to determine if your prospect is a visual, auditory, or kinesthetic. One is by watching the way they move their eyes when they talk or listen to you. The other is from the words they use, which give away their thought processes exactly.

I had a visual a couple of years ago. It was easy to determine he was a visual. He said, "Kerry, I love to read *Playboy* and *National Geographic*, because both magazines have pictures of places I ain't never going to get to."

Visuals' minds work like a picture encyclopedia. They understand what you say by making images in their heads. They have a big picture book up in their heads, and when you start talking, they move their eyes up, and they start flicking around in the pages until they get the one you're talking about. When they get that picture, they make eye contact again. If they can't get the picture for what you're saying, they may never make eye contact.

Basically, visuals do three things with their eyes. Number one, they will typically look directly up to the right when thinking about future information: "I wonder what my wife will look like if I tell her that I bought this product." They'll move their eyes directly up to the left when thinking about past information: "What did

VISUALS
A Visual will move his eyes . . .

Up Right—Future

Up Left—Past

Unfocused

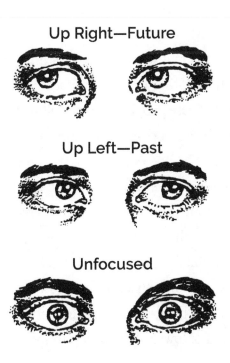

she look like before when I brought something home to her in the past?" Or their eyes will be straight ahead in an unfocused way, or will actually look past or through you.

Have you ever noticed that when you're talking to people, they'll suddenly look just to your side, or through you? They're really not looking at anything. These are visuals. They're thinking visually. They're making pictures in their minds.

You've heard of all the CIA and FBI efforts to find traitors in our government? They can't use lie-detector tests with everybody they come in contact with. They have to have a quick and dirty way of determining if someone is lying or not. Do you know how they do it?

They look at the way their listeners move their eyes. If they ask a person, "Are you smuggling arms to Iran?" and this individual looks up to the right, they're constructing, thinking ahead to the future. They're lying.

But if this individual moves their eyes directly up to the left, they're probably recalling or trying to search their minds from past information. These people are likely telling the truth. That's a great way to determine very quickly if someone is telling the truth or not.

Visuals also do unique things with the words they use. They say things like, "Can you *show* it to me?" "That's a pretty *bright* idea." "I can *picture* that." "It's pretty *clear* so far." "*Looks* good." "Hey, I *see* your point."

When I was in school, the teachers didn't know how to teach you. When I was in third grade, my teacher said to me, "Kerry, what is the capital of Iowa?" I looked up to the ceiling, visualizing what the capital was. Then she'd say, "Kerry, the answer is not on the ceiling." Ever hear that? But the only way I could think was to look up at the ceiling. I got lousy grades that year, and I fault my teacher for that (not me, of course).

Have you ever heard in sales-training programs that you have to keep good eye contact? In fact, visuals are the only people that care about eye contact. Nobody else cares. Here's what visuals will say: "I can tell just by looking at your eyes that you're a sincere guy. I get a lot of trust, a lot of warmth just by looking. I can tell that you're an honest man just by looking at your eyes." But if you're a nonvisual, you may not know what that means or even what visuals are looking at.

I was a stockbroker once for Kidder Peabody. Stockbrokers are taught how to get 400 rejections in the space of one hour. It's called *tenacity*. They build in perseverance. They also make you lose your hair fast. Now stockbroker agencies teach you how to do great things over the telephone, but you're very weak doing face-to-face contact. That was the way it was when I was a stockbroker.

One day I was at that 390th phone call, and I talked to a pharmaceutical CEO. After I asked him if I could see him face-to-face and talk to him, he said, "Yes, I'll come into your office tomorrow from 12:00 to 12:15."

"Wonderful," I said. "I'll see you then." I hung up the phone, went back to my manager, and said, "Steve, I'm going to see this guy face-to-face. What am I going to do?"

"Kerry," he said, "all you have to do is keep good eye contact. Keep good eye contact." It was the only way he knew how to sell: keep good eye contact.

When the CEO came in, I was sitting on one side of the table—really the wrong place to sit for big hitters. You never sit across the table.

He looked at me, I looked at him. I had a set number of questions to ask. I said, "What is your portfolio like today? What stocks and bonds do you currently possess?" Then I looked up at him, and he looked directly to the side, as a visual does. I kept hearing my manager say, "Keep good eye contact."

I moved my chair around to the side. He moved his eyes the other way; I moved my chair around too, until finally he said, "Son, you're making me dizzy. Can you sit in one place?" The point is that visuals are the only people that only care about eye contact.

Often visuals have very fast, high-pitched, voices. They breathe higher in the chest, up near the top of the lungs. Also, they tend to be good spellers. Were you good at spelling in school? If so, chances are, the way you constructed words was to look at each single letter in your mind. You could actually picture the whole word. People who were bad at spelling thought of words phonetically. They heard the way it should sound, and they messed up on the spelling.

Here's an exercise. Take your hand and put it over your wristwatch. Now I want you to tell me right now: what is the color of the face on that wristwatch? Do you know?

Now what are the numbers on that watch face—digits, no numbers at all, just a 12, or frankly, you just don't know?

Number three, what are the colors on the hands of your watch?

Now look at your watch. See what you got. You look at your watch forty times a day. Visuals would probably never even admit to not knowing all those questions.

Visuals are deeply affected by color. Have you seen some of the current color research? Have you noticed that certain people are emotionally led by color combinations? Women have known that for years and years, but here's some of the current research.

A *60 Minutes* newscast once showed how they tried to find out what colors give strength and weaknesses. The experiment was done in a California prison system. They had a guard do as many curls as he could possibly do in the space of ten minutes. I think the guy cranked out twenty-six curls on his own.

They then put blue in front of that guard the whole time he did the curls. He did one less; he did twenty-five curls. Fatigue set in. They then put pink in front of him. Guess how many curls he did with pink in front of him. Five curls. It went from twenty-six to twenty-five to five. You know what they're doing now in the California prison system? They're now putting in pink prison cells. They have them in almost all the maximum-security prisons. When a prisoner goes crazy, they stick him into a pink prison cell for about thirty minutes.

Would you like to hear what the three most sales-stimulating colors known to man are? Number one is hunter green. The second-best color happens to be blue, deep navy blue. The third-best color is gray.

You may have thought that red would be one of the best colors you could wear or have in front of your prospect. Actually, red has been shown to be an enormously good color, but red is sometimes overstimulating.

Here are the three worst colors that you could possibly have. Number one happens to be purple. The second-worst color is pewter green. It's a very dank, dark green. The third worst color is yellow. That's because when you get to be over fifty or fifty-five years old, the brain doesn't register yellow as well as it does in younger people, so it tends to irritate the eye muscles. Another awful color is black. Black—even a blue that's so dark it makes people think it is black is an extraordinarily bad color to wear. Why? Because black symbolizes, guess what, death and dying.

Research shows that the colors you have in front of you when you eat have a great deal of bearing on your appetite and how much weight you put on. If you have red in front of you, it's an appetite stimulant. Blue in front of you is an appetite depressant.

If you know a prospect is a visual because their eyes go up to the sides or they go directly to the side, unfocused—in other words, they're not looking at anything, they're just looking through you—or if they use any of the words I'll list below, they want you to talk to them using exactly the same words. Here's how to communicate with visuals in the way they want to be communicated with.

1. Use visual predicates—words like *show, clear, picture, bright, see.* One woman who made more than $1 million a year in commissions said this to her prospects. If she knew the prospect is a visual, she'd say, "What do you see yourself accomplishing as a result of being with me today?" You could see their eyes go way up at the top. They would look at the ceiling, and they gave her the answer according to exactly how they're thinking.

I can't emphasize enough that if you can get your prospects to think in their most natural mode, they're going to think much more quickly, and you're going to get trust much faster. You're going to get meaning and intent, and you're going to get more business.

I'm going to tell you a cute story about how I found out some of this stuff. When my son, Neal, was ten years old now, and my daughter, Stacy, was two, Neal was very jealous of Stacy. Every time he went by Stacy, he would bump her. He would knock her down, she would cry, mom and dad would get upset, and Neal didn't know what he'd done. He'd deny it even if you caught him red-handed.

"Neal, did you hit her?"

"No, I was in the other room, Dad. No, not me."

"Now, Neal, tell me something. Did you make her cry?" Of course he'd deny everything. I said, "Neal, you can't do that. She cries, I get upset, Mom gets upset." I gave him his first psychology lesson: I said, "Neal, you bump Stacy, I bump you."

He didn't understand that. His mind was off someplace. He said, "Dad, I want to go play baseball."

But as soon as I said, "Neal, when you bump her, is it clear to you that there are tears dripping down her face when she cries? Do you see the bruise on her arm when you bump her? Can you see these things happening?" you could see his eyes light up. "Oh, yes. I get it, Dad. I understand."

The kid was still cocky. He said, "Dad, now I know why grandparents and grandchildren have a common enemy."

Another point about visuals: these individuals deeply want you to watch what you wear. Don't wear any black. As often as possible, wear blues and grays, and reds if you possibly can.

Also avoid dissymmetry. I did a sales conference once. I happened to be wearing a jacket with flap pockets, and one flap was in the pocket, but the other flap was outside. This is dissymmetry.

I got done with my program; it was an hour-long speech. I went to the back of the room, and a woman came over to me and said, "Kerry, I really liked your program. I thought it was a wonderful speech, but I was so distracted for the first fifteen minutes of your talk. I was looking at that flap on your jacket and I couldn't pay attention to anything else you said."

Now I think that's pretty silly stuff, but if you're a visual, you can see how that woman would be distracted by the dissymmetry in my jacket flaps. Think of how distracted your prospects could be if there's something in dissymmetry about you while you're talking to them.

Here's the most important part: you have to let visuals *see* your ideas as often as possible. Draw pictures. Let me give you an example of this. John Savage, who is from Toledo, Ohio, does millions of business each year using the simplest, most unsophisticated technique the world has ever seen. He sells whole-life insurance. He talks to prospects about forced savings plans, and how does he sell those plans? He says, "Mr. Prospect, sir, you're paying *this* much in taxes. Let's see if we can get you to pay *that* much in taxes." Every time he talks, he divides circles, he does bar graphs, pie charts, all of it. It's not really John Savage who is doing the job; he's getting his prospect to see his point so clearly that they understand it twice as quickly. John Savage is a visual too; I think John just sells to visuals.

Here's the last point: use your hands when you talk to visuals. Can you get them to see things by painting pictures for them in the air as well as on paper? If you can, you're probably going to get more business. Visuals want to see it. They want you to use your hands.

One successful underwriter is Russ Gills in northern Virginia. Here's how he closes his visual prospects. He draws pictures, does all the right things, but he also says to his prospects, especially when selling disability insurance, "What do you think your wife is going to look like when you tell her that if something happened to you, she'd have $8000 a month coming in? What do you think she's going to look like?"

What are they going to say—"Oh, she's not going to like that at all"? He's going to evoke a response. In other words, they look up to the right, up to the left, something, but he's going to get them to visualize it, see the point.

Now let's try an exercise. Take an individual; let's call him Clark. I ask, "Clark, can you remember your first car?"

"Oh, yes."

"Tell me about it."

"It was a green 1951 Chevrolet, two-door; it was a stick shift. You'd shift up here, and I had it about eight weeks, and the transmission went out. So I remember that car very distinctly. I bought it in Kansas City, and I drove it to St. Louis, where I was stationed at that point. My wife-to-be was living in Kansas City."

"What did that car sound like when you drove it?"

"When I first drove it out, I started it, and it was clean and all that, so it sounded good. I thought, 'This is a smooth-running little machine.'"

"What did that first car feel like when you drove it?"

"Neat. Behind the wheel of my own car. I'd borrowed cars, used the parents' car and all that sort of thing, but now I had my own car."

Now guess what mode Clark thinks in. It was a green '51 Chevy, and he started painting a picture about the details of what that car looked like.

I asked, "What did it sound like?" and he told me it was clean. He was storing nothing in the auditory mode. That means that Clark is not an auditory.

How about kinesthetic? When I asked, "What did it feel like?" he said, "Neat. It felt neat." Then he started saying what it looked like again.

So Clark is a visual. It is easy to determine this stuff. What if you could do that quickly? What if you could tell if your prospect was thinking visually, auditorily, or kinesthetically? Would you do a better job getting that person to trust you? Would you increase your closing rate?

Two

Auditories: How Does It Sound to You?

The second group are the *auditories*. These people listen to the way you say things. Sometimes they get more information from what you say and how you say it than from anything else. The way you deliver things—the voice pitch, pace, timbre, intonation—means something to these people. They will listen more to the delivery than to the content or the logic with which you say it.

Auditories basically do three things with their eyes when you talk to them. They give you these cues to let you know they're thinking auditorily. They do things like looking directly, straight across to the right, when thinking about future information. "I wonder what my wife will say to me if I tell her I've gone for this product." They look directly off to the side. "I wonder what my vice president of sales is going to say when I tell him I got this product." The third thing they'll do is directly look down to the left. These are what we call *tonal auditories*. These individuals make

AUDITORIES
An Auditory will move his eyes . . .

Side Right—Future

Side Left—Past

Down Left

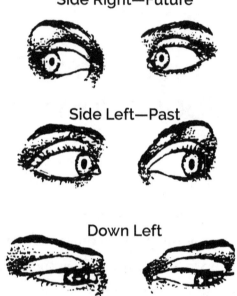

sense out of what you say by talking, having internal conversations with themselves. When they look down to the left, they're actually thinking about what you're saying. They're trying to hear themselves recall what you got through saying.

The movie *Romancing the Stone* was a story about a guy, played by Michael Douglas, who was in Colombia trapping birds. A woman came from New York City to Colombia and had all sorts of mishaps. In one of the opening scenes, when they were both being attacked by the Colombian state police, she was in back of him. He was shooting at the Colombian police and mumbling to himself, "Wrong place at the wrong time."

That's a tonal auditory. These individuals have little internal conversations. They talk to themselves: "Hi, Susan. How are you? I'm fine, Susan. I think I'm doing OK. How's your day going, Susan?" We used to think that was a sign of schizophrenia until we learned that that's an easy way to go through a psychodrama in which you're actually playing out things. You're hearing your own words played back to you, and you resolve problems much more effectively and much more quickly.

Auditories' minds work like those old jukeboxes. When you put a quarter into the jukebox, the little arm would come up, go to the place where the records are, find that record, take it out, pick it up, and put it on the platter. The arm went down, then the record would start going. You got music.

That's how auditories' heads work. They look to the sides or down to the left until the arm finds the right record. When the arm puts the record down and starts playing it, then they make eye contact again.

Auditories use expressions like this: "Don't take that *tone* with me, young man." (My mom used to say that to me when I was young.) "All she gives me is a lot of *static*." "Yes, I *hear* what you're saying." "Hey, that *rings a bell*." "*Sounds* good to me." "Say, did you *hear* the one about the two ostriches?" These individuals are thinking auditorily.

Auditories love to telephone. They sometimes get more business done on the telephone than anyplace else. They have deep, resonant voices. Auditories love the way things sound, and they will certainly listen to the way you say things.

Auditories try hard to sound good almost all the time. In fact, their voices are pitched and paced so that whenever you talk, they can listen to the sounds, and they can reflect those same sounds. Auditories also try hard to make their voices low, rhythmic, and smooth—very low, booming voices.

These individuals like concerts, music. If I gave you the choice between a big-screen television set and stereo speakers on your existing TV, which would you pick? Auditories would rather have better sound coming out of the TV than a better visual image on another TV.

One more thing about auditories: they listen so deeply to what you say that sometimes just the inflection of your voice can distract them. I got a chance to do an agency meeting in Los Angeles with a company called US Life. It was an all-Filipino agency. English was their fourteenth or fifteenth language.

I said to the agency manager, "I'm a little bit nervous. I don't know if I'm going to say things too quickly, if I'm going to say the right things, if they'll understand what I have to say. Frankly, can you help me a little bit?"

The agency manager said, "Kerry, it'd help a lot if you used a Filipino word in saying hello."

"Great," I said. "Tell me what it is."

He told me a Filipino word meaning *good morning, good afternoon, good evening, how are you doing*? I kept practicing it in my head. I kept hearing the word.

The announcer introduced me, and I got up to the front. I said the word. They smiled, and didn't say anything. No laughter, no clapping, nothing. I went back to the back of the room after the program was done, and the vice president came up to me, a woman. She said, "Kerry, I loved your program. Very effective, good presentation, but frankly, I'm a little bit concerned. You know when you said that word?"

"Yes, I practiced five times."

She said, "You told 423 Filipinos that you hope all their pigs die." The littlest inflection in voice sometimes means the most with these individuals.

The best thing that you can do with auditories is use auditory predicates. "How does this *sound* so far to you, Kurt?" "Jim, does this *ring a bell* with you?" "Can you *hear* your prospects saying this sort of things?" "Does this *sound* OK to you, Dave?"

Here, by the way, are the twelve most persuasive words that you can use with your prospects and clients:

Discovery	New
Easy	Proven
Guarantee	Results
Health	Safety
Love	Save
Money	You

You hear these words guess where in our society? Radio, TV, even newspaper advertisements. In fact, you'll find five or six of these words on every piece of correspondence or sheet you get from me.

Auditories are deeply affected by what they hear, so why not tickle their ears? The famous evangelist Robert Schuller didn't have to use overhead transparencies. He didn't have to grab your attention by drawing things. He would say, "What the mind can conceive and believe, it will achieve." Doesn't that sound good?

My life insurance agent says, "Kerry, man, you don't know anything about life-insurance products. Kerry, if you die without enough insurance, you're going to leave your wife feeling financially dejected, abjected, and rejected."

My financial advisor says, "Kerry, you're an economic idiot. Partner, you have to understand simple economics. When your outcome exceeds your income, then your upkeep is your downfall."

By the way, Ronald Reagan was auditory. His nickname was the Great Communicator. Do you remember how he disarmed news reporters? A reporter would ask, "Mr. Reagan, what are you going to do about taxes? Are you going to increase taxes? Are you going to lower them?"

Reagan would go, "Ha, ha, ha. There you go again, Chuck," and everybody would laugh. He would disarm them just by making his noises. That's an auditory characteristic. To the American public, this phrase means, "Don't pull that crap on me. I've heard that before. I don't believe it." Actually James Baker taught Reagan to use that phrase, beating Jimmy Carter for the first presidential debate in 1980. Reagan was spontaneous, but he was a little too spontaneous at the wrong times. If he didn't have a script in front of him, sometimes he'd foul up.

Auditories really want you to tickle their ears. They identify more with this than anything else. If you see prospects and clients in your office, research has shown that you can relax your prospects by playing classical music in your office while you interview them. They'll tell you things they sometimes wouldn't tell other people.

Here's what one underwriter in Southern California used to do. I think this is a great idea, but only for auditories. He would send an audiotape out with the background of his company and some testimonials from his past clients. Think of that. If they could hear it, would they be more easily persuaded to go for it? At least he would develop credibility more quickly.

Listen to yourself very carefully when you talk to auditories. By the way, have you ever had the chance to listen to a recording of yourself? What does your voice sound like? Most people will say, "Different."

What if you're talking to a person who has a higher or a lower voice than yours? That's a mismatch. Your voice is not the same as that person's voice. Wouldn't you get more trust and more rapport more quickly if you could match voice, pace, timbre, and pitch with that prospect? Probably.

The last thing is explaining illustrations the right way. Visuals get more information from what they see than what they hear. Here's what visuals want from you. They want you to give the illustration to them. Don't say another word until they make eye contract again. Right? Then talk about it if they want to.

On the other hand, auditories get more information from what they hear than what the see. Correct? So auditories want you to give the materials to them and let them see the outline to try to get a reference point, but they want you to explain it to them.

Give the illustration to the auditory and wait twelve seconds. We have looked at eye movements. We have mapped out that the auditories will look at the stuff across the top, they'll look at the stuff down the left side of the sheet, and they'll look at a few things in the middle of the sheet, but they will not try to read the sheet or get more information than that from it. Why? Because they get more information from what they hear than what they see. With auditories, wait twelve seconds, and then explain what they just got through seeing.

I was sold some health insurance from what may have been the worst salesperson in the country. This guy happened to sell me, I think, because the product was basically the perfect product for me. I had to ask the man during the middle of the presentation, "What does this thing cover? What are the benefits?"

I was sitting on one side of the room, and my wife was sitting on the other. The gentleman was on the couch directly between us, clear across the room. He was making every mistake in the world. I said, "What does this thing cover? What are the benefits?"

He took out the brochure the company provided him, and he started reading the back of the brochure. Now I loved that because I wanted to hear it. Do you know what your spouse looks like when they can't stand somebody so deeply that they're lathering at the mouth? Her eyes starting rolling in the back of her head. After I signed the contract, she took the policy and said, "Let's go try to place it with someone else." Could that ever happen to you?

Auditories and visuals each want to be treated in a very special way, and it's important to know which way this is, especially with your spouse. If your wife or spouse is a visual and you're a nonvisual, there may a problem there in the way you communicate. When I go home after a long time on the road, all I want to do is kiss and hug. My wife doesn't like to cuddle. She likes to look good. She likes to have nice things. She likes to see pretty objects and things. I like to touch. I like to kiss.

Three

Kinesthetics: Get in Touch with Your Feelers

The last group that I want to discuss are kinesthetics. I call these people *kinos* for short. These individuals decide from the way they feel. They get more from touch, feeling, emotions, gut instinct, visceral attitudes and ideas than they do from the things you say or from the content. They use expressions like, "Hey, partner, let's *touch base* next week." "Let me see if I can *get a handle* on that." "How does that *grab* you?" "It *rubs* me the wrong way." "Here's how I *feel* about it."

Visuals will say things like, "Here's my *view*." Auditories say, "Here's how it *sounds* to me." Kinesthetics say, "Here's my *feeling*. I want to tell you how I *feel* about it. Here's my *impression*."

Kinesthetics move their eyes down one way. They look down directly to the right. Ever heard the expression, "He was downright mean"? Yes, kinesthetic. Down to the right—evoking some sort of response.

KINESTHETICS
A Kinesthetic will move his eyes . . .

Down Right

A guy said to me once, "Kerry, I frankly don't like to sell to kinesthetics. They don't think the right way. They're slower. They're not very intellectually bright people."

That's not true. Einstein was a kinesthetic. In every TV interview he did, when he was asked about E=MC2, where did his eyes go? Down, and most of the time to the right. He would rarely ever make eye contact with the camera. He looked down to the right.

By the way, Einstein came up with the theory of relativity in the space of two hours. Do you know how he did it? He imagined what it might feel like—kinesthetic, feel like—riding a bolt of lightning throughout the universe. Bright people? They're certainly not dumb.

Kinesthetics will give you cues to whether they're kinesthetic or not very quickly. Number one, they feel hot or cold about you very fast. There is a book called *Contact: The First Four Minutes*. It will show you how people will get more information from you and make more judgments about you in the first four minutes than they will in two or three weeks.

Number two, kinesthetics have frequent pauses in the conversation:

"Frank, I'd like to know what you think about what I've just said so far."

If Frank is really kinesthetic, he'll pause. "Well, Kerry, I think that—what you're saying to me right now has a lot of merit, and frankly that—I feel that I—can grasp your ideas, and—" Do you know people that talk like that? They pause in the middle of the conversation. They're trying to get a feeling. "How do I feel about what he just said? Well, it feels OK. I think I'll continue . . ." and they go along. That's actually how their mind is working. They frequently pause.

These individuals also love to touch people. They love to touch things. Sometimes they get more information from what they can touch and feel and tactilely perceive than from what they can hear or see. These individuals will probably touch you to make points. They'll touch you on the arm. They'll touch you on the sides. And when they're feeling good, they can understand and perceive things much more quickly than other types.

Being kinesthetic can have its own problems. During the 1984 election, Geraldine Ferraro and George Bush faced each other in the vice-presidential television debates. The consensus among news broadcasters was that Bush was more charismatic and more articulate in front of the TV camera than Ferraro, although I believe that Ferraro was better informed about the issues.

Bush won the debates basically because Ferraro made some big mistakes in front of the cameras. When the reporters would ask questions, Bush would look directly to the side of the camera and look back again, like a visual, and then answer the question.

What would Ferraro do? She'd look down to the right and completely lose eye contact. I heard Dan Rather and Morley Safer on the CBS coverage. Rather said, "Morley, how comes she's looking down so much?"

Morley Safer said, "I don't know, Dan. There are no notes in front of her. She's not reading anything." Hey, she was a kinesthetic. That was the only way she could think—by looking down to the right. Then she looked back up into the camera and answered the question. But the country didn't realize this. They thought she was trying to hide something because she looked away, down to the right, so often.

When Jimmy Carter was president, he would touch people. He'd go to the reporters and touch them. He used very kinesthetic predicates: "Here's my *feeling* about that." Kinesthetics like to touch people. They like to touch things.

Here's how kinesthetics want to be dealt with. Number one is the same theme that's been running through all the types we've been talking about. Kinesthetics want you to use kinesthetic predicates. They want you to say, "How do you *feel* about this?" "What's your *impression* about what I'm presenting so far?" "Can we *touch base* on this if you have any questions?" "How does it *grab* you so far?"

If you do the same thing, you're going to grab their emotions out of their head. You're going to get trust because you're communicating better with them than anybody ever has in the past. Use kinesthetic predicates. Use a probing question, like, "How do you *feel* about your job?"

An insurance salesperson might say, "If something happened to you, do you *feel* you'd want to provide for your family?" Or "How would you *feel* if we got your premiums down?"

Number two, give kinesthetics things to touch. If you can get them to touch, feel your ideas, you're going to sell them five times as quickly.

I spoke at a major sales meeting in Savannah, Georgia some years ago. I was met a guy on the way to dinner the night before. He said, "Kerry, you're a pretty big hitter, aren't you?"

"I don't know about that," I said, "but I try to do the best I can."

"A dollar means a lot to you, doesn't it?"

"Well, yes, I work as hard as anybody else does for a dollar."

"Kerry, you probably pay too much in taxes."

"Boy, you got that right."

"You work really hard for a dollar," he said. "Give me a dollar."

I didn't want to do this with him. I wanted to go to my dinner. But I gave him a dollar.

"Kerry," he said, "every time you make a dollar like this, the government looks at your hard-earned buck. They glare at you with a mischievous grin that the IRS has. Kerry, they then take that dollar bill, and they slowly in front of your eyes, Kerry, rip up your dollar bill, and your stomach starts churning in the middle of the rip."

The guy didn't have to rip up my dollar, but he got me to feel what he was talking about.

Another time, when I was flying to Portland, Oregon, I sat next to a prosthodonist. Prosthodonists put false teeth in your head. He said, "Kerry, we had enormous problems in our profession. Every time we put a false tooth in, we could expect a life expectancy of about five years for that tooth, and then the gums would atrophy and the tooth would fall out. You'd have to reimplant a new tooth. But now we use titanium. It is such an incredible metal that the fibers around the jaw will wrap around the metal. It will never fall out for the rest of someone's life."

He had that metal right in front of him the whole time he talked. "Wow," I said, "what a hot idea." I reached for it three times. He pulled it back from me three times and kept talking.

I said, "How come you didn't let me touch it?"

"I didn't know you wanted to."

Now what if you can get your prospects to feel what you're talking about? Will they buy more quickly?

You may ask whether you can be a mixture of all these three types. Yes and no. You have one primary mode, and you live in it most of the time. If I leave you alone, if I let you do anything you want, you will probably be either a visual, an auditory, or a kinesthetic. Just by being human, you have the ability to go in any of them if you want to, but it won't be very comfortable for you. You will also have a second most comfortable mode.

If you are a visual, you may be less effective in selling auditories or kinesthetics. But if you can become more flexible with your prospects, you may be able to increase your sales productivity and work smarter instead of harder.

Four

Rapport

Sharp salespeople say that if you apply rapport, opportunities will come to you, and favorable situations will present themselves because of your unique abilities with people. If you have poor rapport, people will avoid you like the plague. This is true in almost everything we do: business, marriage, and one-to-one communication.

Rapport is a relationship marked by harmony, conformity, accord, or affinity. It is the bridge that helps your listener find the meaning and intent with which you say things. If you do not achieve rapport with a prospect first, you may as well shake hands and leave. Without rapport, you're only communicating information; you may as well be reading aloud. The best way to generate rapport is to genuinely and sincerely care about what your prospect needs or wants.

You've obviously realized by now that if rapport is too high, you may end up doing more than just business. You may be entering a very personal or even romantic relationship. If, on the other extreme, rapport is too low, nothing at all will happen.

A million-dollar producer once mentioned that when a client resists him, he knows rapport is too low. He also said that it's a statement that he, not the client, is doing something wrong. If a prospect resists, it only means that the producer hasn't yet found a method of making contact and establishing rapport that his client can identify and work with.

So we need to be flexible when we present ourselves to clients; if we have that flexibility, we have more tools to use with clients. Until we get the rapport response that we want, we are not treating the person the way we should.

I was at a cocktail party a couple of years ago. A gentleman and I were talking about his business. He didn't seem very interested in our conversation, even though he kept talking to me. His business revolved around pipeline hardware for oil companies. While he talked to me, he refused to make eye contact, and he turned his head from side to side while looking around the room. Rapport was tremendously low. I found myself getting more angry and upset the more I talked to him. I caught myself and realized that maybe I was doing something wrong in not grabbing his attention sufficiently, instead of thinking about how much that person was offending me.

My daughter, Stacy, has her own way of dealing with someone like this. If I'm having a conversation with my wife and Stacy wants me to listen to her, she will walk straight over to me and get my attention by grabbing my face with her hands, twisting my face toward her so that I am looking straight into her eyes. At that point, she has my total attention. How often I wish I could use Stacy's technique in my business!

In this chapter, I'm going to suggest some verbal rapport techniques such as matching key words and phrases. You're going to be able to match predicates, you're going to learn more about active listening, and you're going to find out how to reinforce interpersonal trust and generate higher rapport by using small talk.

You'll also use nonverbal rapport techniques. You're going to learn how to match voice quality, pace, pitch, and timbre. You'll learn to identify nonverbal cues and become adept in a technique called *nonverbal mirroring*.

Active Listening

First, here are some verbal strategies you might be able to use. Number one is *active listening*. The first and most obvious rule of active listening is that you should not interrupt your client when he is speaking. Second, you should maintain good eye contact, although not to the point of having a stare down. Third, don't take a lot of notes while someone is speaking; instead jot down an occasional key word or phrase that will help you recall the conversation later on.

The most important goal of active listening revolves around getting your prospect to sell himself because you've generated so much rapport that the things you say are twice as meaningful to him.

There are three stages of selling to highly sophisticated people. The first stage is when you, the salesperson, are very new and try to talk people into doing the things you'd like them to do. When you have more experience, you listen for openings and arguments in which you try to talk them into doing things you'd like them to do. But when you're experienced in dealing with people, your client will talk himself into doing things you'd like him to do simply because you are such a good listener.

One of the best ways to actively listen people into doing the things that you'd like them to do is to play back or repeat the information they said to you. In this way, the client knows that you understand or at least have heard what he has said.

For example, a friend of mine told me this story about a woman who approached him. He said she had stood there in the middle of a restaurant and stared at him. I said, "Stared at you?"

He said, "Yes. After a few minutes, she said she hadn't seen me since the mid-1960s in Paris. All this while my wife was sitting next to me."

I said, "With your wife sitting next to you?" This simple act of playing back key words, or actively listening, showed him that I was interested in his story and thus increased his trust in me.

People have often commented on what a good listener I am. I used to think this was a weakness. I've often thought if I did not share my views and ideas more frequently, people would not be as interested in me, but I found that people care more about what they have to say than what others have to say.

Instant Replay

If you could find out how your prospects think, if you could discover their buying strategy and their hot buttons in two minutes, would it help you sell? Here's another question. Do you believe that the way people bought before will typically predict the way they'll buy in the future?

Typically the way to determine if somebody will buy in the future is to ask them how they bought in the past. Here's what I want you to say. There are three variations. Use them verbatim, word-for-word. Don't judge it. Try it first.

1. What made you decide to buy this (blank) in the past?
2. How did you decide to buy this in the past?
3. Why did you buy this in the past?

If you're selling equities or securities, your client may say things like, "I bought it because of the track record. I wanted to see results. They were company names I recognized."

Now think for a second. If you know exactly those buying strategies that your prospect used to buy in the past, and if you played that back to them, would they have a better chance of buying in the future? If they said no to you when you replayed what they wanted in the past, to deny you, they would have to deny themselves.

I once spoke to a financial planners' symposium. A gentleman who owned a bank management consulting company was also a speaker at that meeting. After his presentation, I saw him in the coffee shop at the hotel and had a cup of coffee with him. I listened to him while he told me about approaching banks and showing them how they could make more money by underwriting junk bonds. While he was talking, I listened intently and played back his key words constantly. During the ninety minutes that we spoke, I said almost nothing except for reinforcing his comments.

A month later, he called me up and said he was the program chairman for the Young Presidents' Organization, an enormously powerful group of young men between the ages of eighteen and forty-nine who owned their own companies valued at more than $10 million. When I asked why he picked me as a speaker, he told me that he thought I was very wise and articulate, and the young presidents could learn a lot from me.

This invitation was particularly curious to me because he found out almost nothing about me during our conversation. Yet we had incredibly high rapport. Because I listened to him so intently and used this verbal playback strategy, he developed a strong bond with me.

One word of caution. People use certain habitual words to generate superficial rapport. The use of these words is almost automatic in our society, but they generate very little rapport. Habitual, automatic words and phrases like *how are you?* or *how's it going?* are generally useless for this purpose.

When was the last time you said, "How are you?" and the person actually told you how they felt? If someone had a cut on his finger, and you said, "How are you?" he'd probably respond, "Fine" instead of saying, "I have a cut on my finger." You say, "How are you?" to somebody who's noticeably sick with the flu, and they'll say, "Great. I'm fine." Or how about this? You talk to somebody who just got hurt in a baseball game or working on their car, and you say, "Are you OK?" They almost always will say, "I'm fine." What else are they going to say? It's a quick, impulsive, automatic question that gets an automatic answer.

If you want to use one of these triggers to develop rapport, try something called *reframing*. Say something like, "Is your day going OK?" or "Has your day been productive?" or "Are things going smoothly for you?" This will get the person to think about what you've just said. When they think about what you've just said, it shows caring, and when you show you care, you're going to get more rapport. Obviously, the greeting should be good enough to cut the ice.

Some people are adept at small talk to generate rapport while others seem to have a really tough time. Which are you? A study done by Harvard University shows that husbands have a very difficult time socializing after their wives pass away, but wives are better able to make the transition after the death of their husbands. The reason? Psychologists find that husbands have not developed the ability to engage in small talk, nor have they developed enough close relationships where they can get on the telephone and just chat with friends during the day as wives often do. Men have a lower acceptance of using this verbal strategy than women.

Sometimes small talk is compulsory. When I call home during a trip to tell my wife what I've been doing, I can't tell her about business until about five or six minutes into the conversation. If I talk business immediately, she thinks I don't care about her or the family, but if I ask about how she's doing or how she's feeling and show concern at first, then I will have generated enough rapport that I can also talk about my business later. In other words, I have to make deposits in the emotional-rapport bank before I try to make withdrawals.

One of the best ways to generate rapport and trust is to use a technique called *matching* or *mirroring* the listener or prospect's key words and phrases. Even though there are more than 300,000 words in the dictionary, most people use only about 1 percent of them. People also have a subset of those words that hold special meaning for them and which they use to convey things or communicate a message.

If you identify and use those key words and phrases, you will have the key to unlock their minds. For example, a popularized mode of communication has evolved out of the San Fernando Valley in California known as valley-girl talk or valley talk. A valley girl might saying to another friend, "He was gorgeoso," or "I thought it was incredibly tubular. It was such a primo idea."

When my son Neal was little, he would use words that were particularly meaningful to his age group. For example, *rad* meant *incredible*, *gnarly* meant *tough* or *difficult*, and *gay* meant *strange*—not homosexual, just weird.

Adults also develop key words, slang, in much the same way. You've heard expressions such as *a rip-off*. He was *a tiger*. *Laid-back*. *Tough*. *A piece of cake*. When most people use key words, they will pause just before and just after they use them; this is called *marking them out*.

For example, a realtor I know listened very hard while a prospect described what he wanted in a property. After talking for a few minutes, the prospect said, "What I want is an—incredible—view." When the realtor heard the word *incredible* marked out, she asked on the spot what it meant to the prospect. And when she showed him the house that had the kind of view he wanted, she reinforced the benefit by marking out that key word: "Tom, here's the house that you talked about, and I think that you will agree with me that you are looking right now at an—incredible—view." Not only did it have a good view, but using that word had special meaning to her prospect, because it grabbed his emotions rather than just communicating information. She got him to think in terms of what he really wanted rather than what the realtor thought he wanted.

A life-insurance agent recently told me a story about a meeting he had. He took my ideas and tried to understand his prospect's vocabulary, especially the key words and phrases. He listened intently while probing. His job was to uncover his prospect's financial needs. In listening, he heard the wife say that she wanted protection with an increase in income as an investment.

These were not words that the agent had learned to associate with the products he sold. He was accustomed to saying "security with income protection." However, he decided to try my suggestion and mirrored what that wife had said. "I understand that you want protection with an increase in income. So here's how this product works."

You see what he did? He reused the same words that were meaningful to the prospect's wife. He didn't try to change her way of describing what she wanted, but instead adapted to the words that she was already comfortable with.

During the first five minutes you're with your prospect, it's crucially important to listen to the way he says things, especially the key words he uses. Note these expressions and the meaning he attaches to them. For example, I don't like to be called a motivational speaker. To me, a motivational speaker is a rah-rah hype, a no-content, no-message speaker who pumps people up and leaves them with nothing to walk away with. As far as I'm concerned, they convey no information, give you no tools, and teach you no skills to use after the meeting, but if one of my prospects says they want a motivational speaker, I'm not going to change their terminology and say, "Sir, I'm not a motivational speaker. I'm a high-content sales psychologist." Instead I'm going to use their terminology, their words, because in their mind, that is what they want. (I have found that generally any speaker who is not a company insider, who delivers a nonproduct, nontechnical speech, is pigeonholed as a motivational speaker.)

If you listen closely to your prospects' phrases, you're going to be able to communicate in the way they want to be communicated with. Make sure to write down these key words or phrases as they talk to you so that you can match their words and phrases when presenting and closing. Above all, use these words and phrases on your prospects at every opportunity.

I recently called a vice president of a stockbrokerage firm on a referral. His name was Jim. I listened well and talked about twenty minutes by phone with him. As he said good-bye, he signed off with, "Whatever you do, Kerry, do it well, have fun, and do plenty of it." Guess how I signed off on a letter that I later sent to him. By mirroring his key phrase, even in a letter, I picked up one of the easiest sales I ever made.

As I've already noted, possibly the best way to establish rapport through verbal communication is to use *intermodal predicates*. These are the types of words your prospect may use depending on whether he is a visual, auditory, or kinesthetic.

Visuals say *see, shortsighted, picture, clarify, perspective, view.* When you talk to visuals, use words and phrases like, "Do you *see* what I mean?" "Can you *picture* this?" "Is this in *perspective* with what you wanted?" "I don't want to be s*hortsighted* with you." "Let's try to *clarify* this first."

Auditories, on the other hand, use words like *tell, ring, key, shout, sound, voice.* To auditories, we need to say things like, "*Tell* me what you like." "Does this *ring a bell*? "Am I *on key*? "Does this *sound* good?" "Have I *voiced* your concerns adequately?"

Kinesthetics use words like *touch, handle, impact, tangible, impress.* Like visuals and auditories, they want you to duplicate or mirror their predicates. They want you to use expressions like, "Let's *touch base* on this next week." "Does this have any *impact* on you?" "How does this *impress* you?" "Am I giving you a *handle* to grab this with?" "Is this *tangible* so far?"

If you use the words most familiar to the mode in which your client thinks, you will get them to process information at the highest possible speed while engaging their emotions at the same time. You're going to get them to think in terms of the natural computer-system language in their heads, which is the best communication style possible.

Matching Voice Quality

You can cut down on the time it takes to sell by increasing the rate at which people respect or trust in your competence. You need to match not only the voice timbre, the pitch, the pace, but also the quality with which people say things.

About one year into my speaking career, I spoke in Birmingham, Alabama. I was thirty minutes into my hour-long program when a gentleman in the back row raised his hand. Not wanting to detract from my program and cut down on my time, I ignored the guy. Unfortunately, he kept his hand raised for about seven to ten straight minutes. He started distracting people around him.

I finally acknowledged this gentleman, and I asked if he had a question. He sat back in his chair, put his thumbs in his belt, and said in a very loud, Southern drawl, "Son, I'd like to know what you said after you said hello."

Obviously I was speaking too fast and had very little rapport. If I thought I was getting the message across to this gentleman or any other people in the room, I was sadly mistaken. I was just wasting my time. The only way I could have said less was to speak longer or faster.

Recently my wife and I decided to buy disability insurance. A health-insurance salesman had approached my wife. His name was Roy, and he asked to come over to our house to tell us about the disability policy he had in mind. I didn't have an opinion about him one way or the other until he came over to the house. He knocked on the door and proceeded to speak very, very slowly, too slowly for me, and inarticulately. He stumbled on words, had difficulty even pronouncing some words.

Unfortunately, he didn't possess the vocabulary I expected from a professional who was going to take some of my money and trade it for a product. In fact, the rapport was so bad between us that I even tried to improve it by slowing down and mispronouncing words as often as he did.

One of the best methods you can use is to listen intently to your prospect for the first three or four minutes and make a mental recording of everything you hear. Listen to their word inflection patterns. Listen to the number of words they use in a sentence. Even listen to how they mark out key words. This information will help you sell them subliminally by duplicating their voice patterns, the words they use, as well as their own nonverbal actions.

People who make their living by telephone prospecting have to be masterful in matching key words and phrases. The way they say things is crucially important, because the person at the other end of the telephone never has the benefit of seeing them face-to-face.

A professional speaker I know in northern Florida has a secretary who up until a couple of years ago felt very nervous, if not panicked, when speaking to New Yorkers. However, she found that when she spoke a little more quickly than her normal Florida drawl, used some New York slang terms, and put more of a New York staccato in her voice, she got more business.

When I'm speaking to people from the South on the telephone, I will often say, "Y'all," and add a little Southern drawl to my voice. The funny thing is, they very rarely ever comment about my accent, because people expect you to talk the way they talk. When you mismatch or you don't communicate in their normal style, you're the one who is causing the tension, not them.

Recently, I spoke to a group in Lake Charles, Louisiana. The audience was composed of life-insurance salespeople who were Deep South Southerners. They had a very slow style of speaking and a very down-home attitude. Another speaker on the program was from Southern California (as I am). He spoke much too fast for this audience. I suspect he didn't have any idea of the mismatching that was going on or of the low rapport and trust he was creating with the people he was speaking to.

I, on the other hand, prepared for this program by listening intently for the first five to ten minutes when a Southerner spoke to get an idea of how fast he spoke, how high his voice was, and the words he used to express himself. I purposely matched all those things as I addressed the audience to try to gain as much rapport with them as possible.

Mirroring

Mirroring is a nonverbal, subliminal technique that will reap rich rewards for you in getting people to do what you'd like them to do. People tend to do business with or put trust in people that are most like them. If you are too much unlike your prospect, it will take longer to build the warmth, trust, and rapport necessary to make a sale.

One way to promote trust and rapport is to mirror body movement and posture. For example, I recently spoke at a sales conference in Northern California. The morning before my presentation, I had breakfast with another gentleman who was also a speaker on the program. While we had our coffee, I didn't say a single word. I just listened and of course mirrored his body movements. I crossed my arms when he crossed his arms. I crossed my legs when he crossed his legs. He said he enjoyed my company so much and felt we had developed such good rapport that he asked me to speak to his company on communication skills. He had no idea that I had simply been mirroring all of his movements to create the rapport he enjoyed so much.

Mirroring or matching body movements is really a by-product of having incredibly high rapport. You see it in friends. You do not see it in enemies, though. Adversaries will deliberately, though often unconsciously, mismatch. If one person has his legs crossed, the other person will uncross his. If one person has his legs uncrossed, the other will cross his. In fact, they often break eye contact rather than try to create any sense of rapport. You often see this in husbands and wives who are not getting along. Often if a husband and wife would simply match each other's movements, they would be in a romantic dance. It's impossible not to be in high rapport when you're sitting alike and moving alike, which promotes thinking alike.

Have you ever noticed that your friends frequently cross their arms the same way you do when sitting with you? They will lean towards you in what we call *cordial unison* when you're talking to them.

In fact there is an old legend among Swiss clockmakers that if you put a room full of grandfather clocks together, in a couple of years they will synchronize their pendulum swings and swing together. The bottom line is, if you can mirror your prospect or listener's posture and physical movements, you're going to have high rapport. When you have high rapport, you have higher trust. When you have higher trust, you have more business.

I recently heard a story of a consulting psychologist who was enormously skilled in these techniques. She was called upon by a realtor to help her negotiate a fee that was due her by a past employer. Apparently the realtor had sold a few properties and earned $10,000 commission, which the broker employer was unwilling to pay. To cloud the matter even more, there was some discrepancy over the actual commission that had been negotiated.

The psychologist attended a meeting between the realtor and the broker. Immediately the broker said, "What's she doing here?"

The realtor replied, "Oh, she's just a consultant I decided to bring in."

The broker said, "This is between you and me, but she can stay as long as she doesn't say a word."

During the entire negotiation, the consultant mirrored and matched body posture with the broker. After about forty minutes, the broker conceded and agreed to pay the realtor $10,000, exactly the amount of money that was in question.

During the meeting, every time the broker said something positive or conciliatory to the realtor, the consultant would match his posture. Every time the broker would say something negative or counterproductive, she would mismatch his body posture.

The funny thing was at the conclusion of the meeting, the broker said to the consultant, "It's too bad you had to sit silently through all this." Obviously the broker didn't even realize the enormous power she had wielded over him simply by matching and mismatching his movements.

Mirroring is very effective, but it is even more beneficial to recognize it as an indication of extremely high rapport. If your prospect is in your ballpark and has rapport and trust in you, he will keep matching your movements. If you say something that that prospect doesn't like, though, or if you lose rapport, that prospect will mismatch your posture. This is extremely useful in determining what people like and don't like when reading their minds.

In the past example, when I talked about the insurance agent selling disability insurance to my wife and me, I purposely tried this. I broke rapport. I crossed my arms and crossed my legs to see exactly what he would do. He didn't change a single thing. His presentation stayed the same. He kept going along the same track, not even realizing that I had changed my mind and was becoming very negative. If you see your prospect breaking rapport suddenly, this is an obvious sign that you're barking up the wrong tree and simply making it tough on yourself.

Crossover Mirroring

I recently had a salesman write to me who said that he was nervous about mirroring his prospects' exact nonverbal gestures for fear that they would think he was mocking them. I suggested that the salesman could do something called *crossover mirroring*, but only if he was very sophisticated and elegant.

Crossover mirroring is taking one nonverbal gesture and doing *almost* the same gesture, but with a different part of the body. In other words, if your prospect crosses his arms, then you cross your legs. If your prospect has his head in his hand, then you touch your chin. If your prospect has his hands in his pockets, then you fold your hands in your lap very close to your pockets. This is enormously effective. It will increase rapport very fast. Likewise, if you decide to change, such as to stop rubbing your chin or crossing your arms, chances are your prospect will mirror and stop also.

Leading and Pacing

Rapport is like money. With it, opportunities begin to appear; without it, you'll go broke. Nevertheless, you should only use rapport as a check to make sure that you are following an effective communication process. A much better way to use rapport, once you have it, is to persuade your prospect and getting her to commit to your ideas. You can utilize the benefits of rapport by leading and pacing.

For example, a flock of geese will fly together in formation. If the lead goose deviates and flies a little left, the rest of the geese don't go right. They don't go straight. They follow in tight formation behind the lead goose.

When you're in rapport, you have incredible power. If you move, chances are your prospect will move his body or posture in the same way that you do. For example, I once spoke at the state meeting of the Texas Junior Chamber of Commerce. That evening before the program, the president asked all the speakers to get together and discuss the next day's presentations.

Before the meeting started, there was a cocktail party, during which I became involved in a conversation with the director of the national JC organization. His name was Tom. Tom and I sat and talked, and I made sure I mirrored him. I crossed my legs in exactly the same way he crossed his. I made sure that my arms rested on the chair in the same fashion his did. I found out that as I was discussing something, when I smiled, he smiled. We kept a very tight formation of rapport, and trust was very, very high.

Then I noticed something very interesting. After about fifteen minutes, I decided to uncross my legs. Within ten to fifteen seconds, he did the same thing. He uncrossed his legs and mirrored me instead of me mirroring him. This is a great way to determine if you're in high rapport, because your client will follow your lead if the rapport is effective.

Million-dollar producers are incredibly good persuaders, and they start by getting very high rapport. They sit the same way their prospect sits. They move the same way the prospect moves. Then after a short time, the prospect starts moving in *their* direction, towards *their* line of thought, both verbally and nonverbally.

Recently I visited a financial planner's office in Appleton, Wisconsin. In the middle of the meeting, I noticed that his client was sitting all the way back in his chair. The planner, whose name was Frank, stayed back in the same basic position, leaned forward, and talked about the goals he had for that meeting. His client, in the meantime, leaned forward as well. You could see they were off to the races with high trust. Closing the client successfully and getting a sale at that point was almost a shoo-in. It was as predictable as night and day. Frank knew that if he could get his prospect to sit forward, his prospect would increase his enthusiasm. Do you smile because you're happy, or are you happy because you smile? (Hmm.) Frank knew that if his prospect sat forward, it would affect his behavior.

Good speakers, especially motivational speakers, will use this technique with large groups of people. They will match and mirror body posture for a few minutes and then lead the group to do what they want them to do.

I recently watched a motivational speaker at work. As he was introduced, there was a round of applause, but he noticed that the audience was sitting back in their chairs with their arms crossed. The speaker crossed his arms at the podium and spoke in a fairly low-voice volume, trying to match and mirror the group. He even put his hands in his pockets. (This is an of crossover mirroring.) He matched and mirrored the group verbally. Most importantly, as the presentation progressed, he used his hands a little bit more to illustrate ideas. He modulated his voice and gradually grew more excited and enthusiastic.

He did some pacing and then tried to lead the audience. He paced them by making statements such as, "You're incredibly bright people, and you probably know this idea I'm sharing with you is one of the best ideas you'll ever hear." He paced what the group already knew and then led them to do what he wanted them to do.

You have already read about the effects of verbal pacing in leading. One reason so many of us agree with people who comment on the uneasy subjects of politics and religion is that they first make a series of statements that nobody can disagree with, and then give you their unique philosophy or viewpoint. We find ourselves agreeing with that philosophy because we are in such high rapport that we feel unable to break it.

I received a direct-mail piece for a seminar. The cover said, "You are reading this flier. You are looking at the words. You are thinking, 'Is this worth it?' You will get ideas to help you increase your sales by 100 percent in the next three weeks."

The flier was designed to pace the reader by making undeniably true statements such as, "You are reading this flier. You are looking at the words." It led the reader into a new line of thought once the reader had some moderate level of rapport with the written copy.

On an airline ride recently, a gentleman sat next to me and found out I was a psychologist. He said, "You sound very articulate, and you probably have a good marriage, and you probably know how to deal with people including your wife and your kids." He paced me so well through all these statements that he slid me into his leading statement and said, "With all your knowledge of psychology and human behavior, you probably realize how difficult women are to get along with, especially after the first two or three years of marriage."

Now I know of no research that has determined that women are more difficult to get along with after two or three years of marriage. In fact, in my own marriage, my wife was easier to get along with after two or three years. Nonetheless, I caught myself agreeing with his statements because he had paced me so well. He led me to the thought patterns he wanted me to have.

Some salespeople will use pacing insincerely. They will use pacing in telephone prospecting techniques by saying things like, "Mr. Prospect, you're a very bright man. You understand life. You understand economics. That's why you'll buy this sixty-inch TV set for $699, because you realize it's such a good deal." The prospect says, "No, I don't realize this is such a good deal. I'm going to give you three orders. Hang up, don't call back, and leave me alone."

The key to using proper pacing is something so simple that a ten-year-old can do it. It is easy to make undeniably true statements that the listener believes and agrees with. However, the most important aspect of pacing is that *the prospect must feel that you are sincere in your statements*. Slowly pacing or leading that person into a new line of thought is called *deduction*, but it is more from an emotional level than from a factual one.

Now that you know something about verbal and nonverbal pacing, would you like to see how easy it is to lead and pace people once you have established rapport? Here's an experiment you can try in restaurants or coffee shops.

Pick out a table in which the person has a view of you or is at least facing in your direction. After sitting there for a few minutes, mirror that individual. If he has his head in his hands, put your head in your hands. If he's crossing his legs with the right leg over the left, you do the same. If he has his head cocked to one side, mirror that.

Then, after a few minutes, change. Try to move your head to the opposite direction. Take your head out of your hands. Put your feet flat on the floor without crossing your legs. Even though that person is not sitting at your table, it's very likely that if you have done an adequate job of mirroring him, you can lead and pace him to mirror you back to keep rapport. This is enormously funny to watch.

Think of how effective this could be. You could actually change your prospect's comfort level by getting rapport first and then mirroring the right way. Here's how to do it.

Number one, make sure that you duplicate whatever posture your prospect takes during your meeting with them. If they cross their legs, cross your legs. In other words, get nonverbal rapport very quickly. When you sincerely feel that rapport is becoming deeper and deeper, generate more enthusiasm and higher attention in that prospect by slowly leaning forward. Uncross your legs. Put your forearms on the fronts of your legs. You can generate enthusiasm in that person by leaning forward, which should cause him to lean forward as well. But if you determine that that prospect isn't leaning forward like you, retreat back, then start from ground zero. Try it again.

Recently I received a letter from an insurance salesman describing how he had used this technique on a business owner who was very difficult to communicate with. The owner would constantly sit with his arms and legs crossed during their conversations and his presentations. The salesman couldn't get anyplace. The next time they met, he used my idea of matching and mirroring the business owner during the first twenty minutes of the meeting. After the twenty minutes was up and rapport was fairly high, he leaned forward, hopefully leading his prospect to generate enthusiasm and excitement about his ideas.

The business owner, who previously was so difficult to even get to talk, suddenly displayed trust and rapport. He leaned forward with my salesman friend, nodded his head when my salesman friend nodded his head, showing very high levels of rapport and the desire to stay in rapport.

My friend said, "Kerry, I couldn't believe what happened. All I know is that I closed him. The man wrote me a check for $25,000, $12,000 of which was my commission for that day. Kerry, I wish I had used your techniques fifteen years earlier. I could have made ten times the amount of money I'm making right now."

Breaking Rapport

Establishing and gaining rapport is important, but breaking it may also be necessary from time to time. For example, have you ever had a salesman in your office and felt like telling him to leave, but you didn't because you felt it was not polite? Or in the middle of a nonproductive meeting, you felt like leaving, but you felt it would be gauche for you to say, "I'm not interested in this anymore. Time's up. I'm leaving." What if your prospect becomes too talkative, going off on tangents while you're trying to sell him? He wants to discuss politics or religion. You would probably find it difficult to say to him, "Let's go back to the subject at hand," or, "Hey, let's stay on track."

How do you break rapport with people without appearing rude? By now it should be apparent how easy this would be. You can break rapport without someone even realizing that you have terminated the conversation or redirected the topic.

For example, I spoke to a prospect recently. We were talking about sales training, and the prospect suddenly started discussing other problems he had with his staff. His problem was that the secretaries were demanding more money from him. He underpaid them. I had initially gone to see him about doing training for his sales group. He wanted to talk about getting his secretaries to work harder even though he underpaid them. I realized this was a dead-end street. We could have been there for three hours and without fulfilling my agenda for this meeting. So, I decided to break rapport.

He and I were both sitting forward, talking about his staff, when suddenly I sat back and went so far as to break eye contact.

He kept talking but realized unconsciously that my interest was waning. He hesitated and paused. I redirected the conversation back to sales training and thereby kept him on track.

This may sound to you a bit abrasive or rude, but this gentleman did not sense it. He only perceived that the conversation was being redirected. He did not consciously realize that I broke rapport.

One of the best ways of break rapport is, plainly and simply, to mismatch body posture. Do *not* mirror. If they cross their legs, uncross yours. If they lean back, you sit forward. If they talk slow, speed up.

I once knew a manager who knew exactly how to break rapport with telephone salespeople. During the conversation, he didn't feel as though he wanted to be so rude as to say, "I'm busy, call me some other time." Instead he tapped the telephone with a pencil while the salesperson talked. Obviously, this distracted the telephone salesperson so much that they became unnerved. The manager told me that this technique was almost 100 percent effective.

Rapport breaks are often used by businesspeople to sabotage meetings. For example, in the middle of a meeting between a salesman and several key business executives, one or two of the executives will purposely mismatch and break rapport after it has been established. They don't want to see it culminate in a sale.

I talked to a salesman recently who was selling a financial product. The decision maker had matched, mirrored, and kept high rapport throughout the interview, but when it came time to close, the decision maker broke rapport. He leaned back in his chair and avoided eye contact. In counseling the decision maker, the salesman found out that the decision maker was afraid of facing his own death and wanted to avoid discussing anything about it.

Still other people break rapport with you only because they unconsciously want you to pursue rapport with them and try to get it back. For example, women in their early twenties will sometimes use a very interesting and simple technique called *teasing.* The woman will match and mirror a male very closely. When the male crosses his legs, she will cross hers. She'll lean forward when he does. She will match his voice tone, pace, and pitch. During a conversation, she will even match his words. Suddenly, as if by lightning, she'll break off all rapport, cross her arms and legs, leaving the male feeling totally mystified. He sincerely thinks he has done something wrong and will try to gain rapport back. He'll lean forward and pay more attention to her. He'll act almost as if he is pleading for his life. Women use this technique in order to trap males and get them to commit themselves more to a relationship. Many women use it, and believe me, it works like a charm.

Before I got married, I dated a woman named Gail. Gail had a wonderfully pleasing personality and was very friendly and athletic and easy to get along with. Gail was enormously attentive as well. I noticed on our second date that she did all the right things, mirrored, matched, smiled frequently, and kept good eye contact, but in the middle of dinner she broke rapport. She tapped her fingers on the tabletop. She even went so far as to cross her legs and arms.

I found myself instinctively leaning forward and trying to regain rapport by being more humorous and witty. I found myself complimenting her more. I tried to regain eye contact. In other words, her use of rapport-breaking techniques was manipulating me into committing myself more to her.

Anchoring

Would you like to make people more receptive to you when you talk? Would you like to change your listener's attitudes and emotions while you sell? Would you like to get people to understand you without having to say anything verbally?

I recently walked into a Nordstrom's department store to buy a new suit. A good-looking saleswoman came over and talked to me for a few minutes about what I wanted. I told her I wanted a gray, double-breasted, pinstriped suit in a 41 long. As soon as I spoke, she spontaneously touched me on the arm and said, "Hey, you're awfully good-looking." I felt complimented. She never said it again, but she showed me four suits and was able to close me so effectively that I bought two of them on the spot.

Here's how she did it. As I walked through the store, she said, "Hi. My name is Sally. What's you're name?"

I said, "Kerry." We chatted for a few minutes about the store and the overall suit selection.

Then she touched me on the arm and said, "You're awfully good-looking."

"Thanks," I said. She took me to the clothes rack and picked out four suits in my size.

After fifteen to twenty minutes of trying on these suits, she closed me by saying, "These two look great on you." She then touched me on the arm in the exact same place she had touched me before. I felt the same good, warm feelings as when she initially said, "You're awfully good-looking." In other words, she anchored me with her touch on the forearm, and I bought the suits. This was such an elegant way of getting me to buy something that I not only bought those suits, but I've gone back to her to buy most of the suits that I now own.

As I said, Ronald Reagan was a masterful communicator. He frequently got tough questions from reporters about his administration. During the 1980 debates, when Jimmy Carter accused him of being a warmonger, Reagan smiled and chuckled and said, "Ha, ha, ha. There you go again." Throughout the whole campaign, as soon as Reagan smiled and chuckled, he never had to say, "There you go again." The country came to know what that chuckle meant. This is called *anchoring*. During press conferences, Reagan would use a chuckle—"Ha, ha, ha"—to diffuse very tough questions by causing laughter from the whole audience without even saying a word.

One of the most effective ways of dealing with people is to anchor them in their matching emotions. Anchoring is defined as the technique of bringing back memories and emotions by using verbal or nonverbal cues or changing someone's attitude while you're communicating in a subliminal but effective way.

You can generate instant emotional response just by using a couple of quick techniques. You see, we attach meaning to other things besides words. For example, two fingers up in the 1960s meant "peace." One index finger up during a sport competition means number one. During most business meetings, raised eyebrows mean surprise.

We anchor emotions by giving cues. Most of the cues you can use with individuals as anchors are unique, exclusive, and individual. You can create new, nonverbal messages and influence your prospect or listener by associating even a single word with that anchor.

For example, at a sales meeting recently, I was in the middle of the conversation with a manager. We developed rapport. We talked about tennis and golf and traveling on airlines. When I felt rapport was at the highest possible point, I touched that manager on the arm. After about forty minutes, I presented my ideas and tried to close him. I again touched him on the same place on the arm. He was all over my ideas like a cheap suit.

The best way to use anchoring is to anchor emotions when rapport is at its peak. You touch, smile, point a finger, raise your eyebrows, or any nonverbal body language gesture that can be associated with that moment of trust. Then you can bring that trust or rapport back instantly by using the same touch, smile, or finger raise that you used in the first place.

Here's another example. In the middle of a conversation, a financial-planner friend of mine asked his client, "What is the most important aspect of tax shelters in your philosophy?"

The client said, "Well, I guess security is the most important thing to me. I don't like to take risks." When the planner repeated back the prospect's desire for a shelter with low risk, he raised his eyebrows. In other words, he anchored his prospect visually.

During the presentation about mutual funds, he had an idea that was right for the client. The planner said, "Mr. Prospect, this Oppenheimer fund will give you high growth, and it's a tax shelter with low risk." He raised his eyebrows. The planner could see his prospect's eyes light up.

The prospect smiled and said, "That sounds great to me. Let's go ahead with it right now."

If you really want to create commitment, you can use anchoring to control your prospect's emotions and change the level at which they respond. It's simple to do. The most important thing is to try it. Ronald Reagan anchored by smiling when he was discussing very touchy subjects. You associated the smile with past good feelings, and it made controversial subjects seem less dramatic.

At one time in her career, the great comedienne Joan Rivers made an incredibly funny joke out of the expression "Can we talk?" Years later, as soon as she said it, people would roar with laughter, because she had anchored emotions to that expression. On the old *Tonight Show,* Johnny Carson had a golf swing which meant, "We're ready to start." He never had to say, "Let's go"; you knew it because he had swung his imaginary golf club. The late comedian, Freddy Prinze used to say, "It's not my job, man." Don Schula of Miami Dolphins fame crossed his arms and looked down at the ground, which meant to his players they had better get going.

There is one further step that you can use in anchoring. Some of the most educated communicators and salespeople will anchor in the prospect's thinking mode. For example, if the prospect is a visual, they'll anchor visually. If the prospect is an auditory or kinesthetic, they'll anchor auditorily or kinesthetically.

For example, if your prospect is a visual, he responds more to things he can see as well as view or imagine. With visuals, during high rapport, you would give visual anchors such as a smile, or you can point a finger in the air or nod your head up and down. When you close your visual prospect, you grab his emotions by associating that same gesture with a suggestion to buy.

In my speeches, I visually anchor laughter. I tell a joke or story and broadly smile to initiate an anchor. Later, when I want the group to laugh or chuckle at a subtle line or nuance, I broadly smile again. The group laughs more quickly. It works like a charm.

Auditories respond to things they can hear: the pace, the tone, the pitch, the sounds. They'll respond to sounds like clicking pens, hands clapping, tapping objects, voice inflection. They will even respond to something as simple as the pitch in your own voice. At the point you anchor emotions with auditories, make your voice go very high.

For example, if you say, "Isn't this an incredible idea?" at the point in the presentation when you try to close that prospect, your voice uses the anchor inflection in almost the same way. "Within two years, your profit will increase by at least 25 percent." This reestablishes the emotions your prospect felt when you anchored him initially.

Kinesthetics are probably the easiest to anchor, because these are people who respond to touch. They respond to emotional or gut responses if you can touch them with a pencil or with your hand. For example, when you tell a joke, touch them when you tell the punch line. You will have anchored that emotion, so that when you touch them later on, such as when you are closing them to buy a product, it will bring back the same good emotion that they had when they heard the joke. This is probably the most effective subliminal technique you can use to close your prospect.

Stealing Anchors

Here is another technique that is at least as effective for anchoring people. People possess their own unique anchors. Most people have their own nonverbal communication methods and techniques, which mean special things that are exclusive and unique to them.

Just think. What would happen if you could steal someone's anchors? You wouldn't have to create new ones as long as you knew what the prospect's anchors meant to him. Everybody has certain movements, which means something to them. If you could find out what those nonverbal gestures and postures were, you could use that prospect's gestures and postures back on him.

For example, I spoke at a financial corporation in Cincinnati a few years ago. The vice president of marketing had a very interesting way of shaking his head horizontally from side to side as if thinking no, although actually it meant yes to him. It was a very spooky nonverbal gesture. Even when he and I talked face-to-face, I noticed that when he thought yes, he shook his head from side to side.

When I presented the idea of training his managers, I stole his anchor. When I wanted him to commit to the training, I shook my head horizontally from side to side. It was incredibly interesting to watch his facial expression immediately change to understanding and excitement and hear him say, "It sounds like a good idea to me. Let's start this right away."

The best way to steal anchors is to watch your prospect for four or five minutes and find out what their unique anchors are. Then use them back on the prospect. It's so easy to do. Try it a couple of times to test it.

If you experiment with your prospect and he responds to your anchor, you have it. If he doesn't respond to it, it's probably the wrong anchor to use. Try another one on him. He'll be unaware of what you're doing. Chances are, it'll make a winner out of you in almost any sales situation.

Hidden Commands

We have noticed from viewing and listening to some of the biggest hitters in the sales business that certain phrases seem to generate responses from people. These phrases tend to get prospects to think the way you'd like them to.

Some of the most charismatic leaders in history have been able to lead people to do things they wouldn't normally do. Much of this is based on *trigger words* or *hidden commands*.

In a research study a few years ago at a major university, a number of students were in line waiting to use a photocopier to copy some documents. In one case, a student went to the front of the line and said, "I need to make this copy fast. Do you mind?" In the other case, a student walked to the front of the line and said, "I need to make this copy fast because my car is double-parked. Do you mind?"

Can you guess which worked the best? It was determined that the student who used the key word or hidden command "because" was able to use the copier three times as often as the researcher who did not give a reason or say "because."

You may be thinking that the catalyst was not the word "because," but the reason. However, another study was conducted to test this hypothesis. The researcher walked to the front of the line and said, "I need to make this copy fast. My car is double-parked, and I need to go," without saying "because." Even in this case, the researcher was not allowed to cut in line nearly as often as the researcher who simply used the word "because."

A great sales superstar in the insurance business by the name of Ben Feldman uses some seemingly hypnotic techniques on his prospects called *autosuggestion*. He says things like, "I found that a million-dollar policy was the best way to go for another client of mine whose circumstances were quite similar to yours. Do you see what I'm saying, Don?"

By emphasizing that the million-dollar policy was the best way to go, he gave an honest but suggestive command, which the prospect, of course, received. It reinforced the idea that it was the right thing to do at the right time. Now your prospect probably won't change his mind if you use a negative, but it will reinforce potential behavior and help the prospect make a decision a little bit more quickly.

Other salesman use hidden commands like this: "A month ago, I had a question from a friend who was also thinking of *buying this plan*." In each case when he said "buying this plan," there was a hidden command in the emphasis.

In another situation with a securities salesman, the salesperson said, "Other investors made a quick decision, Steve," and he emphasized the "made a quick decision, Steve." Although you're probably thinking this is a very overt technique, it often works enormously well.

Hidden commands are used frequently and effectively in newspapers and television. You hear television ad salesman heavily emphasize products they'd like you to buy. For example, they'll talk about a popular dog food and say things like, "Spot, as you can see, is going for this Alpo because he loves Alpo," emphasizing it very hard.

It's also used in newspapers and printed advertisements. They will emphasize, or mark out, certain key words or key ideas to get people to buy more quickly because of simple hidden commands.

Five

Finding Outcomes

Joe Gandolfo, the self-proclaimed top salesman in the world, once said, "Find a need and fill it, and you'll make money doing anything you want to do in your whole life."

It's long been said if you can help people get what they want, they'll help you get what you want. This chapter is dedicated to that same altruistic yet profitable idea. Here are some of the things you'll learn from it: (1) how to give your prospect your own outcomes in his unique thought mode; (2) how to get his desired outcomes in his thought mode, or how to get him to let you know what he wants in his most natural way of thinking; (3) how to speed up the sales process and get a deal done more quickly by reaching agreement much faster.

Using this concept, called *outcomes*, is powerful but easy. It's almost too easy. It sometimes takes the challenge out of persuasion. It is diametrically opposed to the type of manipulative sales strategies employed by the old-time salespeople with the white buck shoes and white belt of the Willy Loman, *Death of a Salesman* era. This type of salesman will try to talk you into doing what he wants you to do.

Listening is the most important process in the sales cycle, yet listening alone is not enough to ferret out the unique information that lets you know exactly what your prospect wants.

Recently I bought a car stereo for my wife for Christmas. I walked into the stereo store, and a young salesman, about twenty-six years old, said, "Can I help you?" He blew it immediately by asking an automatic trigger question.

I caught myself saying, "No, I don't need any help. I'm just looking," but I did need help. After about fifteen minutes of looking around, I said to him, "I do need your help. I'm looking for a car stereo."

Then he had the nerve to say, "So you need a car stereo, huh?" and proceeded to show me at least twenty different models, even ones that seemed guaranteed to blow your eardrums apart in thirty minutes—so many, in fact, that he confused me to the point where I walked out of the store without a car stereo. I ended up getting a more thorough education than I wanted or needed. I pretty much knew what my wife wanted in a car stereo. If he'd only had the sense to ask me for my outcome, he would have been able to make a sale instead of educating me more than I wanted and eventually giving the sale to someone else.

Getting outcomes is incredibly powerful but underused. Be careful not to confuse it with understanding needs. Getting outcomes is more powerful than just understanding needs because when you find out your prospect's outcomes, you're understanding not only his needs but also his fantasies. You're understanding his goals and desire as well.

You see, a *need* is what the prospect thinks he wants at the time. An *outcome* is what the prospect wanted in the past, present, and what he may want in the future.

An old sales adage that says, "Give them what they want first, then sell them what they need later." Unfortunately, most people don't know the difference. When you, the salesperson, have enough trust and loyalty, when the prospect believes that you know what they want, then they will trust you to sell them what they really need.

With outcomes, we get both. We find out what they want and what they need. As Henry David Thoreau said, "If you always help people get what they want, be assured you'll get exactly what you want."

This is the five-part process for getting and dovetailing your prospect's outcome:

1. Present your outcome to your prospect.
2. Ask for your prospect's outcome.
3. Use the as-if fantasy technique.
4. Notice their nonverbal responses.
5. Work to dovetail your outcomes together so that it's a win-win relationship.

To use this process, you have to have rapport. If you don't, it will be a mistake to even start to get your prospect's outcomes. It is foolish to think that you can even get close to finding out what your prospect wants when trust and credibility are not yet established, but when you do have high rapport and high trust is established, then present your outcomes to the prospect. Tell him what you want from him. Tell him what your goals are in being with him. Let him know flatly and outright why you're there to see him. Obviously telling him that you want to make $10,000 in commission won't do much for rapport, but if that is the only reason you're there, you won't be much help to him anyway.

For example, John, a realtor said to his prospect, "Mr. Prospect, I'm here to find a property for you that fits your needs, because if you can get a property that you really want, then I can earn commission dollars, and I can bring home the bacon and buy my family the car that is my goal right now." Have you ever given your own outcome to your prospect? Don't be surprised if the prospect increases his trust in you, because honesty is truly enhanced.

Supersalesmen across the country report that their clients feel that the salesman did such a good job for them that they want him to make money and will give him referrals to help him make more money and get more business.

In my business, I often do programs for which I travel clear across the United States for a fairly low fee. I say to my prospective client that I'm willing to come and do that program because, frankly, there are a lot of company executives and meeting planners who will hear me do this presentation. It's a great showcase. It's great exposure for me.

Once my prospect knows my motives and outcomes, he is much more apt to help me accomplish them. To judge from past experience, if I didn't let him know, he would be suspicious; he might even jump to the conclusion that because my fee is so low, I am not a very good speaker or I am going to say something unprofessional.

Number two, find out your prospect's desired outcome. Elicit their outcome. Most interviews start out like this: "As you recall from our phone conversation, Mr. Prospect, we discovered ways of lowering your taxable income. I have a few ideas for you that might help you to achieve these goals."

Unfortunately, the salesperson who uses a line like this has no idea of what the prospect's goals are. If he doesn't know his prospect's goals, he surely won't know his outcomes. If he doesn't have his outcomes, he's doomed to failure. He should have said, "Is lowering taxable income still a top priority for you, Mr. Prospect? Why?"

Elicit your prospect's outcome before doing anything else. It may be the most important question you'll ask the whole time you're with him. Say something like, "Now that I've told you what I want, tell me what you would like to see happen as a result of my services."

Try to phrase the question like this, in a way that helps your prospect, using his own primary dominant thought system, whether it is visual, auditory, or kinesthetic. It will help him think much more quickly. Say something like, "This is what I want. Tell me what you want."

If you're very sophisticated, you could even try to match his visual, auditory, or kinesthetic mode. "This is my goal. Tell me what you'd like to see happen as a result of us doing business," or

"What do you hear the result of my services to be?" Or "What do you feel you want as a result of my services?"

The prospect will tell you exactly what he wants if you use these words in this way. If you listen, you will arm yourself with the best ammunition you could ever have. But if he flatly doesn't know what he wants, he'll say something like, "How should I know? I haven't thought much about it," or "I just don't know what you can do yet. Can you give me more information about yourself?"

People who don't know what they want are often the toughest to sell, because when they don't know what they want, you have to educate them. Sometimes you must even create or illustrate a need that they have not thought of. People who know what they want, or tell you what they want, are the easiest to sell.

The realtor who sold us the house we are currently living in actually found it by knocking on doors in the neighborhood we wanted to move into. We told the realtor that the house we wanted was called a Greenbriar model in Irvine, California. Unfortunately, there were no Green Briars on the market in that community. So the realtor went around door-to-door, on foot, to various Greenbriar owners asking them if they would like to sell their house.

Unfortunately, she made a big mistake. She knocked on doors and said, "I have a buyer that might like to live in this neighborhood and likes the floor plan of the Green Briar. Would you be interested in selling yours?" Out of forty-three Greenbriars in existence, she found only two whose owners who were even willing to talk to her.

This may seem like just good old patience and tenacity, but it was probably closer to stupidity. What if she would have approached each of these various owners and said this? "I may have a prospect who is interested in buying a Green Briar. Have you thought of moving to a different location or needing a different style house? What are your plans for the next five years? Where would you like to live? Have you thought of an investment? Have you thought of houses in other areas?"

Research statistics show that people tend to move every five to seven years. If this realtor could have found out the homeowners' outcomes for new housing, she would probably have picked up two commissions from the same sale instead of just one from us. As it turned out, the people who sold their house to us bought two condominiums with the proceeds of the sale, and our realtor didn't get a penny in commission from them.

The What-if Fantasy

The next step is the *as-if fantasy.*

Is it hard for you to sell people who don't quite know what they want or need? Is it easier for you to sell people who already know what they want? Because then you're not creating a need with the people; you're selling them exactly what they want to fulfill their expectations and goals.

Here's what I want you to say to them. I want to show you the manipulative version first, followed by the technique that might work a little better.

Put them in the future, and have them think back to the past. "Let's assume for a second, Gene, that our meetings are over with. What have I said, or what has happened to let you know that this is the right product for you?" Then you stop and listen. "What has been said, what happened to let you know that this is the right product for you?"

The second version is probably a little more realistic: "What has to be established here so that you can feel that you had all the information you needed to make the right decision?" In this business, the simple stuff sometimes works the best.

One big problem in trying to find your prospect's outcome is that they just don't know what they want. These people are extremely tough to sell, but what if you could ask them a question in which they would give you their outcome? What if you could find out what they want? Would you be able to sell them more quickly?

An as-if fantasy tries to put your prospect into the future with your product. It tries to get the prospect to think ahead one hour or ten years into the future to let you know what he liked about the product, how it helped him, or how he wants you to sell him.

Say to your prospect, "Let's just assume that our interview or discussion has ended. What has happened during this interview to let you know that the time was well spent?" Or "Let's assume that it's six months down the road. What has occurred during that six-month period to let you know that you got a good deal with this?"

You get responses like, "Well, the house we bought appreciated $20,000 in six months. My family likes it, and nothing fell apart." Or if you're selling a tax shelter, your prospect might say, "One year has elapsed, and the tax shelter appreciated 18 percent, just like you said it would." You'll get responses like, "Nothing happened to make me lose money in this deal. That's what I like about it." Or "This company stayed in business to give me a payback on my investment."

Say the prospect says, "The house has appreciated $20,000 in the last six months. My family likes it, and nothing fell apart." In this case, the realtor that asked this question got three very powerful objectives toward selling the house. This is an incredibly useful technique.

You might even find that this is too easy, because if you can get your prospect to do future planning to let you know exactly what he wants from your product or service, and if you give it right back to him, it's like shooting ducks in a barrel. It's like having someone hand you money without your doing any work for it. It makes even salespeople who have no talent enormously profitable, because they're finding out exactly what their prospect's outcomes are and giving it to them. That's because the information you get from this process will let you know what their real objectives or hot buttons are.

This is more valuable than any other probing technique you can use. If you want to be very sophisticated, you might even try matching your prospect's thought mode with the as-if fantasy in getting outcomes. You might say something like, "Let's assume it is six months into the future. What has happened that made you *feel* you got a good deal?" Or "Let's assume that it's six months into the future. What has happened that made you *view* this as a good deal?" Or, lastly, "Let's assume that it's six months into the future. What has happened that made this *sound like* a good deal to you?"

I used this technique with a sales manager for Blue Cross. He was procrastinating in deciding whether to use me for a program.

I quickly realized that I didn't know his outcomes yet. Otherwise he would have booked me on the spot. So I decided to ask him a quick question. I said, "Bill, what do you really want for your salespeople? What is going to do them the most good?"

"Gee," he said, "I'd like them to be more motivated, make more sales calls. I'd like them to work more effectively, work smarter, not harder, and increase their self-esteem."

I realized right there that Bill's analysis of what his people needed was like a wish list stretching from the earth to the moon. His salespeople required everything under the sun. That was as bad as if he had said, "I don't know what they need." He gave me too much information.

I decided to do some future planning or as-if fantasizing with him. I said, "Bill, let's pretend that we completed the program. What happened three to six months after to let you know that it was effective?"

Bill suddenly got very specific. He said, "Well, the salespeople have a higher activity level. They increased their sales by 25 percent, and they have more company loyalty.

From these choice pieces of information, I was able to tailor my comments exactly to what Bill wanted to hear. I gave him testimonials from other companies in practically the same industry that had sales increases of more than 25 percent after my presentations, in many cases, 70, 80, or 90 percent. I was able to show him letters from salespeople who increased their activity by 200 to 300 percent for a period of time directly after my presentation. I even found one letter to say specifically that the salespeople had more loyalty and more gratitude toward the sales manager for putting on such a fine presentation as the one I gave. I got the booking, but had I not used the as-if technique, I can guarantee that it would have taken me a whole lot longer.

Number five, try to dovetail your outcomes. In psychology, a negotiation paradigm that will always work is called *win-win*. The old sales model said that the prospect is the enemy; the salesman is the tough competitor. It was either a win-lose or a lose-win. Some believe that win-lose has always been the case and always will be the case, but the opposite is true: if you let your prospect know what you want, what will make you win, she'll help you win also. At the same time, you have to help her win as well. In other words, you are dovetailing outcomes. You're letting her know you want a commission for a job well done. At the same time, you're going to do your best to help her get what she wants.

Let me give you an example of how this five-step formula works. I spoke to a group called the National Association of Health Underwriters, a health-insurance organization dedicated to helping its members have more education and higher professionalism as well as serving a forum for networking and political activities. The program chairman who was referred to me was named Rod. I'm going to reenact the discussion Rod and I had.

KERRY: Rod, as we discussed, Tim referred me to you
thinking that you might be able to use a sales psychologist
on the next convention program.

Rod: Well, I respect Tim's advice and suggestions.

Kerry: Rod, I want to speak at this convention obviously
because I make a fee, but also because it's the kind of
program I'll get a lot of referrals from as well as getting

more company business. What I really want to know is what kind of speaker you think would fit best in your plans.

Rod: I don't know. I guess a speaker who is well known, who will draw people. I can't see having a speaker do a presentation to an empty room.

Kerry: That makes sense, Rod, but to give me more information on what you want, let's assume that the convention is over. What did you see happen that let you know the speaker was successful?

Rod: Let's see. I see the attendees walking up to me, saying that it was the best convention they ever attended. The speakers were entertaining but informative, and they involved the audience so well that the attendees felt part of the program.

Kerry: Ah, so your view is that you want a speaker who is entertaining and informative and involves the audience in the program. Is that the way you see it?

Rod: Yes, that's exactly it.

Kerry: Good. Let me show you some recommendation letters from groups who said they found each of these three things in my programs.

As you can imagine, I spoke at the convention. I got a bigger fee than I expected. Rod helped me get my outcome and appreciated that I let him know what my outcome was. More importantly, even though he didn't know what he wanted, I got him to do some future planning with me. I found out exactly what his needs and wants were. As the end result, I got a big fee, and I got a lot of referrals. It was the perfect program for me.

By the way, did you notice that when I was talking to Rod, I used the visual, auditory, kinesthetic modes as part of future planning? I tried to match Rod's thinking mode. Did you detect what mode Rod was using? He said, "Let me *see*," and "I *see* the attendees walking up to me." He was a visual. When I talked to him, I tried to help him visualize. I said, "So your *view* is that you want a speaker who is informative and entertaining. Is that the way you *see* it? Let me *show* you some recommendation letters." Use this. It will really work.

I recently talked to a financial planner who used this technique on three business executives. He was trying to get his clients to invest some money. This one technique, the as-if future planning technique, netted him $50,000 commission in his pocket in half the time. Why? Because he found out his prospect's outcomes. He (1) told the prospect what his own outcome was, and (2) he found out what his prospect's outcome was. He used the as-if fantasy. He knew the nonverbal responses as he spoke, and he dovetailed his and their outcomes to support a win-win situation. Use this as-if technique in uncovering outcomes, and you'll have a lot more business than you have right now.

Instant Replay

Would you like to get your prospect's buying strategy? Would you like to know exactly what process your prospect will use in making decisions about your product? Well, it has a lot to do with the way your prospect has made decisions about the products he's bought in the past.

If you believe, as I do, that people will make decisions in the future as they have in the past, then chances are you're going to sell a whole lot more because you probably already know one of the most fundamental beliefs in modern-day psychology—that people typically change very little through the years in their basic personality and behavior patterns.

A great speaker and philosopher named Charlie "Tremendous" Jones once said that you will be the same five years from now as you are today except for the books you read and the people you meet. Car dealers have long known that if you bought a fast sports car in the past, you typically want to buy a car that is fast and sporty in the future.

A couple of years ago, we bought a house that had a big backyard and a fairly large living room. It's amazing to think back about each of the two houses that we have owned. Both have big backyards and large living rooms. It seems as though we gravitated towards looking at and buying houses that are in the same style almost every single time. In fact, when I think back, I even have the same kind of office. I read the same kind of books, and I wear the same kind of clothes as I did a few years ago.

Is it the same with you? Has your behavior pattern generally been the same in the past as it is today? If you could find out how your prospect bought before, would it help you sell him today? If you could, you would learn his buying strategy, and then all you would have to do is play back that strategy to your prospect by using instant replay. Here's how it works.

Ask your prospect a very simple question: "How did you decide to buy this insurance policy before?" Or "What made you decide to buy this insurance policy before?"

This is precisely what an insurance agent said to his prospect a short time ago. His prospect replied, "I bought that past policy because the company was one that I recognized. They promised cash values that would be pegged to the prime rate, and the agent promised me he would follow up at least once a year and stay interested in me."

With these three answers, guess what the insurance agent did. He waited until he got through the probing interview, but guess what high points he focused on when he presented the product. It was so simple. All he said was, "The company has been around for about sixty years. It's a company you should recognize. It pays cash values pegged to the same rate as the prime, and I promise that I will keep in contact with you at least once a year."

A good follow-up question is, "If you did it all over again, what would you improve in this product?" Then you're not only getting past behavior patterns, but also getting a wish list. You're getting a buying strategy from that person, assuming that he will buy in the future as he has done in the past. You've taken the information, and you play it back to them. To deny you, they would have to deny themselves.

But be careful: this instant-replay technique might be too powerful. An insurance agent recently told me that his technique is working so well that practically every single person he meets and makes his presentations to buys his products. He says his closing rate has risen to almost 100 percent. He says he's actually getting lazy, because he knows whenever he sees somebody now, he can sell them as long as they have an IQ above room temperature.

Let me give you an example of how I've used this technique. A broker/dealer in the financial-services industry, whose name was Charlie, once talked to me about doing training for his brokers. In the past, he used a psychologist from Laguna Beach, California, on self-image. When I used this same technique on Charlie, I said, "How did you decide to go with this guy before?" I followed up by saying, "What made you decide to go with him?"

Charlie said, "Well, Mike was referred to me by one of our brokers. Our brokers liked his humorous speaking style and his high content, but also he was willing to prorate travel expenses to our various offices. He was motivating because he told a lot of stories to illustrate his ideas."

I followed up by saying, "What is one thing you would like to improve in the presentation from this guy?"

Charlie said, "I guess the only thing I'd like to improve is to get Mike to tailor his message a little bit more to the specific needs of our group."

This gave me great information on giving Charlie exactly what he wanted. All I did was use instant replay. I replayed the information I'd obtained during the probing or interviewing period. I simply gave him recommendation letters and testimonials that I had from groups who had heard me speak in the past and that thought I was motivating, used humorous stories, prorated expenses, but most importantly, tailored my message to the group. All I needed to do was prove that that was exactly what he wanted, and I got the business.

If you can find out your buyer's strategy, and then replay it to them, he'll give you anything you want, but again, be careful because it's very manipulative if used the wrong way. You can sell people things they don't need and don't want by using too much psychological manipulation. Use it sparingly and carefully, and your closing rate will go to 100 percent.

Psychological Sliding

Have you ever had a prospect or a listener that froze on an objection or an attitude and then became so rigid that you couldn't move him off it? In that situation, a concept called *psychological sliding* may help.

Psychological sliding is a way to move your prospect from one thought pattern to another. It's a way to help him sell himself so that you can pay attention to his thought patterns rather than trying to fight him objection by objection. It's simply elegant and enormously effective while being effortless. It's a way that you can get him to experience the product through more than one thought system.

When I was shopping for cars in a BMW dealership, salesman walked up to me and said:

Salesman: Nice car, huh?

Kerry: Yes, real nice.

Salesman: What do you like best about it?

Kerry: Well, I guess the way it performs, its power and handling.

Salesman: Would you like to sit in it?

Kerry: Yes. I've driven it before, but I'd love to try again.

Salesman: Do you feel you'd like to own it?

Kerry: I think it has a little too much power for my needs. The 528E would probably suit me just as well, and frankly, it's just a little bit less expensive.

Salesman: It really is a nicer care than the 528E. I think you'd feel that you should have bought it in the end.

Kerry: No, no. I think I'll go compare prices on the 528E and give you a call in a few days. OK?

Salesman: That's fine, but just out of curiosity, do you feel that your image is important to you?

Kerry: Sure.

Salesman: Can you see the difference between the 528E and the 535I on the road?

Kerry: You bet.

Salesman: A professional in the public view like you needs to keep up a good image. Right?

Kerry: Yes.

Salesman: I would venture to guess that when you drive to a presentation or a meeting, the attendees get an idea of your level of success by the way you look. Right?

Kerry: OK, but what are you getting at?

Salesman: Since you can see the differences now in the two models, other people, possibly your prospective clients, see them as well. If you could get one or two more clients because of this car's ability to enhance your image, then do you think you could see yourself owning this car?

Kerry: Hmm, well, you bet.

Salesman: Sold.

In this example, the salesman knew that I was a kinesthetic by asking what I liked about the car. My response was power and handling, but he used a valuable technique. He found me objecting to the car because I knew I didn't need that much power. So he slid me into the product and found my hot buttons by asking what else I liked. He trial-closed me kinesthetically by saying, "Do you feel you'd like to own it?"

I gave an objection that it was too much car for the extra money. He tried to counter the objection, but I almost left by saying, "I'm going to compare prices. I'll see you around later."

Then he switched channels, thinking modes. He did a psychological slide to visual by asking me a very visual question. He said, "Do you feel your image is important to you?"

I of course said, "Yes." He started me in the feeling or kinesthetic mode and then slid me into the visual mode to get me to see the benefits of the car so that I would not give him objections in a kinesthetic mode. Then he led me into seeing myself get more business as a result of owning a more opulent car.

His technique would have worked with selling boats, insurance, even pencils. He realized that I was blocking or objecting in my kinesthetic mode, so he slid me into my visual mode. In this situation, as in your prospect's, my visual was not as dominant as my kinesthetic, but it worked as a last resort to move me into a visual to get me to stop thinking so hard about the objection.

There are three basic steps in using this technique effectively:

1. Psychological sliding starts with matching your client or prospect's focus of attention. Match or pace his attention by say-

ing something like, "Isn't that a nice car?" instead of making the big mistake that most retail salespeople make by saying, "Can I help you?" or "Can I help you look for something today?" In other words, don't be too abrupt. Slide, don't jump.

2. When you sense that your prospect is blocking with an objection, slide smoothly to another sensory focus, for example, from feeling to seeing, from kinesthetic to visual. The objection may not exist in another mode. For example, if they say, "*Looks like* it's too much for me," instead you say, "Do you *feel* that you'd like to own it?"

3. Try to help the client experience the new mode as much as possible. Using this you might get the prospect to experience the visual of the car in talking about how nice it would look in his driveway or how it would look to people when he drives down the street in such a gorgeous new car. All of these visual images should conjure up a desire to own it instead of giving objections.

Psychological sliding is especially helpful with rigid or inflexible people. Individuals who don't understand the benefits quickly will respond very nicely to this. This is also really effective with indecisive people or those who need to be led a little bit more.

This technique will help you fight objections by using one of the most sophisticated yet easy-to-use principles in sales psychology.

Six

Overcoming Objections

Now I'm going to talk about how to overcome objections subliminally. Have you ever had an objection you couldn't answer? Has your prospect ever given an objection that seemed foolish to you?

In this next example, a health-insurance salesperson will give you a good idea of a poorly handled objection.

Agent: Before I leave, I'd like to get a quick medical history on you.

Customer: Wait a second. I'm really having a problem with the premium price. It's really too much.

Agent: Yes, but it's a great policy. You'll be sorry in the end that you didn't act on this quickly.

Customer: I don't think that I can afford the premium. It's just too much.

Agent: It's really not that much. It's only $20 a day. You can
   handle that, can't you?
Customer: Let me think about it, and I'll get back to you.

Do you think the prospect eventually gave the salesman the
business? If you're thinking no right now, you're absolutely right.
What did the salesman do wrong? Could he have ever cashed this
objection instead of wasting his time?

First, let's discuss what objections really are. Objections are
very valuable in letting you know what your prospect is thinking
and telling you whether you're satisfying your prospect's needs. A
lot of salesmen talk too much and don't listen enough. They never
really know their prospect's needs or desires, because they've
spent their whole time telling the prospect what they have and
how important it is to the prospect, even though they don't know
what the prospect needed in the first place.

Here are a few points to remember when cashing an objection.

1. Do you have rapport? Did you check your body posture? Are
   you voice-matching? Are you using the other techniques that
   you've learned in this book?
2. Do you know your prospect's outcome for the meeting? Do
   you know what your prospect really wants from you?
3. Have you listened well enough to gain information about the
   prospect's needs?
4. Did you match the product benefits to your prospect's needs?
   Don't just list benefits, but give your prospect exactly the benefits
   he needs to understand why the product is important to him.

Here are three steps to cashing objections—to turning an objection into money.

1. Acknowledge the objection.
2. Uncover the intent behind the objection.
3. Resolve subliminally.

First, acknowledge it. Listen carefully to voice cues. Listen to how high the voice is, how low, how soft, how hard it is. Next, pace the objection. Your prospect has a frame of reference in which he gives you the objection. Use your prospect's reference point to start the answer.

For example, I was cold-called recently at my office by a computer salesperson. The salesman walked into the office and talked to the secretary about the computers we had. I walked out of my inner office to see what was going on.

His name was Ed. I told Ed that I had enough computers. I didn't have any other needs, but I told him the gentleman across the hall from me who's a property and casualty insurance agent had a deep need. I escorted Ed into the insurance office.

After the introductions, the insurance agent, George, listened to Ed for about ten seconds. He then said, "Computers are really too expensive for me right now."

To which Ed replied, "It costs you not to have one." Ed missed the whole point. He didn't see past the objection. He mismatched. He was abrupt and too blunt. He should have said, "You're right. They're expensive, but would you agree that in the end, it may be expensive not to have one?"

That's a much more elegant way of acknowledging that you care about your prospect's objection initially. If you don't acknowledge the objection, you get into an ego tug-of-war which you, the salesperson, never win.

Also double-check rapport. How are you sitting? Where are you sitting? Are you within one or two feet of your prospect? Where are their hands, eyes, and arms? Are you matching and mirroring him while he is giving you those objections?

Step number two: uncover the intent and the meaning behind the objection. You have to understand what they are really thinking behind what they say. Listen between the lines. Often the objection is really a ruse covering a fear of giving you the go-ahead, or the prospect just think that it's appropriate to object, that they are supposed to give you an objection, they're not supposed to give in very quickly. In many cases, it's just a fear of change, a fear of making a decision.

From now on, uncover the real meaning, the intent behind the objection, by saying things like, "That's an interesting comment. Why did you bring that up?" Using this one sentence will ferret out the real meaning behind the objection and the real idea behind their words.

For example, as a new consultant, I went to an insurance agency in Los Angeles called Massachusetts Mutual. The general agent there was Bruce. Bruce quickly gave me an objection after he heard what I had to say for a just a few moments. Bruce said, "We just had a speaker recently. I can't use you."

"I see," I said. "Why is that a factor?"

"We just used this guy. He was well liked, but we didn't get any increase in sales. It was just entertainment with no benefit."

I promptly proved to him how insurance agencies that I had worked with could increase their sales. He then said, "Your approach is very interesting. Let's talk some more."

If I had not ferreted out the real intent by saying, "Why is this important to you?" or "Why do you bring that up?" I would have been walking out the door before I had a chance to walk in.

Number three, in answering or cashing objections, test the importance of the objection. Unless you like getting into verbal boxing matches with prospects, you hopefully realize that you're not paid to explain, you're paid to close. You need to find out very quickly if your prospect is committed to solving his own needs. Start saying things like, "Is that all there is standing in your way in going along with this?" Or "If we get past this point, can we write this up?" Or "If I can answer this to your satisfaction, can I go ahead with this?"

If your prospect says no or "I don't know," it's probably just a ruse. He's feeling other roadblocks or dissatisfaction behind the objections he's giving you. He's not committed. Go back and find out what his real needs are. You probably haven't done a good enough job of probing him initially. Go back and reestablish his goals and outcome.

I once heard about a salesman who was with a prospect for almost three straight hours. For ninety minutes of those three hours, he kept answering objection after objection. He probably believed in sales by attrition. He could have short-circuited the whole process after the first objection by saying, "Is this the only thing that is bothering you?" or, "If we get past this, can we write this up?"

If you can't get a commitment like that, go back and problem-solve again. Get more information. Find out what the prospect really wants instead of what you think he wants.

Using Metaphors and Stories

Another way to cash objections is by using metaphors. Metaphors are especially useful in getting your prospect to notice benefits, because you've described his situation in a different way, a way that actually yields him knowledge. A metaphor is a verbal association between a present situation and another situation which helps in the understanding of the initial situation. It tends to generate emotion from the listener. A metaphor gets your prospect to see, hear, and feel himself in the pictures, sounds, or feelings you produce for him with the analogy. Metaphors are not only entertaining, but are far more emphatic and meaningful than flat statements. Hopefully you can get the listener to envision exactly what that idea might look like.

Let me give you an example. During my first years in the speaking business, people often said, "You're a pretty good motivational speaker, but we've heard all those motivational speakers before." That used to make me uneasy and irritated, but I countered it with a metaphor. I'd say in response, "Well, the difference between me and other motivational speakers is like the difference between a BMW and a Pinto. One is definitely more valuable." In this metaphor, I was trying to get the listener to understand that my message was long-lasting and useful.

One motivational speaker I know used to say that he was in the transportation business: he took people from where they were to where they wanted to be.

Here are some other metaphors you'll hear: "He doesn't have a snowball's chance in hell of making it." "That idea will work when donkeys fly." John Madden, of Oakland Raiders fame, didn't say that one of his players was unintelligent. Instead John used a metaphor: "This guy's elevator doesn't go up to the top floor."

Take this one: "That idea will work when donkeys fly." What if somebody simply said, "That idea won't work?" Far less emphatic or meaningful, isn't it? Or saying, "He probably won't make it" rather than "He doesn't stand a snowball's chance in hell." Obviously it's much more emphatic to use these cute little phrases, but more importantly, you're tying the listener emotionally to what you're trying to convey.

Burt Meisel, a life-insurance agent from Detroit, has an uncanny way of using metaphors in the right way in selling whole-life insurance. He listens closely to his prospect's frame of reference and picks out specific metaphors and stories to illustrate the point.

Once he was asked by his prospect, a carpet manufacturer, what the difference between whole-life and term insurance was. Burt said, "To tell you the truth, the difference between whole-life and term is like the difference between indoor and outdoor carpeting. Both look nice, but one lasts a whole lot longer and gives you more benefit in the end."

If you can tailor your message to your prospects' jargon, reference points, and background, they're going to understand your message a whole lot more quickly. I've heard it said that the top sales producers are decorators of the commonplace. They make even mundane things seem exciting and provocative.

On the other hand, trite metaphors tend to be ineffective in evoking emotion and understanding. If the expression is so trite that it doesn't cause you to pause and think about it, it won't grab you as hard, for example, "My hands are tied" or "This will be curtains for him" or "I like his song and dance." Expressions like these are too automatic. They'll evoke a thoughtless response. You want your listener to think about the metaphor long enough to identify with it.

The Power of Stories

Would you like your listeners to think of you as more charismatic? Would you like to get your ideas and points through to your prospect in one-half the time? Would you like to grab emotion from your prospect much more quickly?

It has a lot to do with the way you use metaphors and stories. We have determined that the best-performing salespeople in the country—the people who make the most money—frequently use trite expressions, stories, and metaphors to get their prospects involved in their products. You see, logic shrinks the mind. Metaphors and stories make people fascinated, even with boring subjects. They expand the mind.

Let's turn now to stories. Let's go back to the example about the health-insurance agent and his prospect. You saw the mistakes the agent made. How would he have answered his prospect's objection, knowing the things that you know now? Let's rejoin him in dealing with his prospect the right way and cashing objections rather than letting them sit on the table unanswered.

Agent: Before I leave, I'd like to get a quick medical history on you.

Customer: Wait a second. I'm having a problem with the premium price. It's really too much.

At this point, the salesman checks rapport. He checks body position, his leg position, to match the prospect's. He even makes sure his voice is matching the right way.

Agent: I hear you saying the price is a little bit high. [He focuses on the auditory mode.] Is this a big concern to you?

Customer: Yes. I don't want to pay more than I have to. It's not crucial, but my father-in-law is an ex–insurance agent. He told me the premiums are about $1 per $1000 on coverage for permanent insurance. Yours is five times that expensive.

The prospect is getting a little suspicious because the father-in-law probably bragged about cheap insurance. The insurance salesman suddenly remembers the outcome of this prospect was to get basic protection for his family.

Agent: I understand that cost is important to you. Do you remember that you indicated protection as an important factor in purchasing this policy also? Does that still ring true with you?

Customer: Yes, but I still don't want to pay too much.

Agent: I understand your concern about paying too much for insurance. In reaching my recommendation on the best product for suiting your needs, I took into consideration both cost and your desire to give your family the best possible protection available, but I was worried about one thing.

Customer: What's that?

Agent: I could have used cheaper products from other companies, but I had a family man like you a couple of years ago for whom I got the best price. The insurer eventually went out of business. It was real tough for the client to get the insurance and the premium and policy straightened out. Even though I was there every step of the way, we ended up going to an established company with a great reputation, and of course more realistic premiums in the end. Am I on base in my reasoning?

Customer: I guess my father-in-law is a little bit behind the times.

Agent: Should we get back to the medical history?

Customer: You bet.

If you follow these steps, you're going to get a lot more business, because you're telling the prospect exactly what he wants to hear in the way he wants to hear it. More importantly, you're selling smart rather than knocking your head against the wall.

Metaphors and stories work to make you money in the sales process in four basic ways.

1. You're able to grip the listener's attention so deeply that it is like watching a very dramatic movie. They're listening to emotion, not just to dry facts.

2. Metaphors and stories simplify ideas. Even the brightest people love simple, easy-to-understand concepts.

3. They get your listener's emotions going. If your prospect is at all influenced by his emotions, using metaphors will help sell him. If you can use the right metaphor to get the prospect to see himself in the situation, then he'll go for it, because he doesn't want to make mistakes.

4. Probably the best reason metaphors and stories work is that they are memorable. Your prospect may forget the facts, but he'll remember the stories and the illustrations you used in talking to him. Human beings love stories. It's like the difference between reading a college textbook and watching *Star Wars*.

To the untrained eye, using metaphors and stories looks as easy as a tennis pro hitting an overhead smash, but in effect, it's as powerful as a Howitzer cannon against a .22 pistol.

Try this. During the next two days, whenever you explain something to somebody that might be even remotely difficult to understand, try to create a metaphor or story from your listener's viewpoint. See if you can make that listener understand your idea more quickly with this technique. Try it at least three times today and tomorrow, and see if it doesn't make you much more charismatic to anyone you're communicating with.

Rephrasing and Diffusing Objections

Another way to cash objections is to rephrase them. The objection may turn into a benefit if you reword or rephrase it the right way. The objection could become very useful in satisfying another need. A Cadillac salesman might say, "What do you think of this beautiful car?"

The objection might be, "It's too heavy."

The salesman then says, "Well, it may be heavy, but it has road-hugging weight."

An objection in insurance might be that the premiums are too high. The salesman then reframes the objection and says, "You're right, but high premiums usually mean quality protection. With a family as beautiful as yours, quality protection is just plain smart."

The Westinghouse Corporation has reframed the name of one of their products. Instead of calling it a dishwasher, they call it a "freedom machine." One of my favorite objections in my business are prospects who say, "We don't use industrial psychologists." Now I counter and say, "Do you use sales psychologists?" In other words, I reframe my position to something that they can more closely identify with.

Another great technique is diffusion or dissociation. From time to time, all of us get negative reactions when we try to close prospects. They may give an objection that is irritating.

I remember talking to the vice president of training for a major airline in San Diego, California. After about forty-five minutes into the conversation, it was obvious I had what he needed, and I probably said, "Why don't you give me a 25 percent retainer right now? We'll start today."

What he did give me was an enormously negative objection. He said, "We haven't covered my real needs yet. Now how can you think or suppose that you know exactly what our needs are?"

Obviously I closed at the wrong time, and I dissociated myself from my mistake by saying, "I just wanted to show you a quick example of how some salesmen would close, but I prefer to be a much better listener. I just wanted to give you an example of the mistakes some salesmen would make." In other words, I dissociated myself away from the mistake I had made in the first place.

The last point under cashing objections is simply selecting a solution that answers true needs and stays within the context of the question. If you solve the customer's needs, and if they know that you're solving or filling their needs, you'll end up getting many fewer objections you might expect.

Seven

Tying It All Together

Up to now, you have had information presented in a bits-and-pieces fashion. Below you will find ideas and methods for incorporating all of the techniques into a logical progression. This section will show you how it all fits together.

I once spoke to a group of bankers in Wintergreen, Virginia, a resort near Roanoke. One of the attendees admitted that when dealing with lawyers, he reverts to an intimidation negotiation style that he says he prefers, but after reading this book, you should now know that if your behavioral tool chest consists only of a hammer, you tend to treat everything like a nail. In this section, you will, of course, find ways to use a hammer, but you'll also learn how to integrate the ideas you have read about so that you can say the right thing to the right person at the right time.

Following is a close account of a meeting between a first-time prospect and a financial planner who has become an expert in these subliminal selling techniques. You will get a chance to hear the dialogue between Dennis, the planner, and Chuck, the prospect, along with an analysis directly afterward. Try to do your own play-by-play as you read.

Dennis: Hi, Chuck.

Chuck: Hi.

Dennis: It was nice of Ben Lewis to refer me to you. Have you known Ben long?

Chuck: Yes, for a couple of years. We play tennis together.

Dennis: Oh, that's great. I play tennis too. I think without it, I would suffer from Dunlap disease. That's when your stomach dun laps over your belt.

Chuck: I know what you mean.

Dennis: Chuck, as I mentioned to you on the telephone, I'm a financial planner. Tell me, what does financial planning mean to you?

Chuck: Well, my view is that financial planning is a way to protect yourself from abusive taxes and help plan for future financial needs. Right?

Dennis: Right. You seem surprisingly informed already. It's important for me to know what you think about financial planning in order to give us a place to start out. You obviously are fairly familiar with personal economics. One more question, Chuck. What do you see yourself accomplishing as a result of our meeting today?

Chuck: Well, I envision finding out more about my financial weaknesses and some mistakes I've made, but I also want to buy a new house in the next year. I would like to cover some ways that I can use my money better in making purchases like that.

Dennis: Why do you picture yourself buying a new house?

Chuck: I like the one I'm in, but some friends have said that buying a rental property may be a smart move. What do you think?

Dennis: Well, if you don't mind tying a lot of money up for a few years and you like to spend massive amounts of time managing the property, it could be pretty lucrative. Let's assume that it's five years down the road. What happened that let you know an investment like this was good for you?

Chuck: That's a tough question. I guess the property appreciated 15 to 20 percent every year, I only spent a few hours a month with property maintenance, and I was able to write off most of it on my income taxes.

Dennis: So 15 to 20 percent, little maintenance, and income-tax write-offs are important to you, correct?

Chuck: Yes, I guess.

Dennis: I had a client come in here last week. He had much the same picture of his objectives as you. We first met five years ago, just as you and I are meeting today. He was a teacher just like you. After five years, he is sailing for six months in the Caribbean with his wife and son. Five years ago, he had about as much money as you have now, but he received 28 percent on his invested dollars after taxes because of write-offs and hasn't had to spend even one hour maintaining a rental property. Are you interested in how he did it?

Chuck: You bet.

Dennis: He put his money into what is called a real-estate limited partnership.

Chuck: Now wait a second. I've looked at those before. You stick in a pile of money, and the IRS may just come along and say, "We don't like this when it's too abusive. We're going to disallow the tax benefits." Then I'd be stuck. At least with my own rental, I know I could write off the losses for improvements.

Dennis: I can tell why you think that way. Have you heard about due diligence?

Chuck: No.

Dennis: This is where an army of attorneys and CPAs in my company check out every nook and cranny of the partnership to make sure that whatever the real-estate company promises, they deliver. This is all done to protect you, Chuck. What's your feeling on this?

Chuck: Due diligence, huh?

Dennis: Is this IRS thing the only part that was of concern to you?

Chuck: Yes, but I guess not anymore. But will you guarantee that this due diligence will forestall any problems?

Dennis: Can't do that, Chuck, but let's look at this colored chart showing the track record of this partnership for the last fifteen years. You can see here where it has averaged 30 percent for seven years straight.

Chuck: Yes, wow, that's a lot better than rental property for that time period.

Dennis: One more thing, Chuck. The family sailing in the Caribbean, the reason they did so well is that they bought into the partnership quickly. If you don't mind, I'm going to call in my secretary with the agreement forms to sign so we can take advantage of this investment. By the way, should we meet again next Monday at 3:00 or Tuesday at 4:00?

Chuck: I like your style. This track record shows exactly what I need. Let's meet again on Tuesday, and I'll be right back. I have to go out to my car to get my checkbook.

How many subliminal selling techniques did you note Dennis using?

1. Dennis immediately got rapport by talking about Ben Lewis.

2. He also used humor to relax Chuck.

3. Dennis then asked Chuck what financial planning meant to him to try to find out Chuck's thought mode. Is Chuck a visual, auditory, or kinesthetic? He's a visual. Remember Chuck said, "My view is?"

4. Dennis complimented Chuck to establish higher trust. Remember him saying, "You seem surprisingly well informed"?

5. Dennis tried to find Chuck's outcomes for the meeting by asking what he wanted to accomplish. Did you hear Dennis match Chuck's visual mode by saying, "What do you see yourself accomplishing?"

6. Dennis wanted to get more information about Chuck's outcomes beyond just the desire to buy a rental property. So he used as-if techniques. He said, "Let's assume it's five years down the road." By using this, Dennis found the three key important decision points that were motivating Chuck to buy a rental house.

7. Dennis actively listened and played back these three points as a check on what he had just heard. This also increased trust and showed Chuck that Dennis cared. The three points were: 15 to 20 percent appreciation in property value, few hours spent in property maintenance, and high tax write-offs.

8. Dennis used a metaphor and story to get Chuck to identify himself with a successful investor who was sailing carefree in the Caribbean. Dennis used this story to get Chuck to consider a real-estate limited partnership.

9. Chuck promptly produced an objection, which Dennis answered by using psychological sliding. Chuck's objection was visually oriented, so Dennis slid into the kinesthetic feeling mode at the end. He then used the most important

point in cashing objections: he asked Chuck if he had any other concerns before he went on. This prevented a duel of objections that could have lasted a long time.

10. Dennis showed Chuck a colored graph of the partnership's track record, which Chuck loved because of his need for information he could see to comprehend data better. Remember, Chuck was a visual.

11. Trying to close Chuck, Dennis gave a hidden command. He mentioned that the family sailing in the Caribbean bought into the partnership quickly. Dennis did an assumptive close, rescheduled another appointment with an alternative choice close, and made the sale. The expert planner made more money.

As has been constantly reiterated, these techniques should be used to help your clients rather than just make you more money. Otherwise you'll win a few, but the word will get around, and you'll lose much more than you'll ever win. With these techniques, you'll produce more business than ever before.

A successful financial salesperson who makes $550,000 a year recently told me that if he had known these techniques twenty years ago, he would be making ten times the amount of money he is currently making. But then only the already successful top 10 percent would ever use these ideas. The rest just ignore it and go back to being in the bottom 90 percent. I hope you stay in the top 10 percent.

Roundup

You have learned some of the newest and most successful techniques in sales psychology. Your mind will now work as if it has just had jet engines attached. You will be able to use these techniques even unconsciously, because you have spent hours reading about ideas that you can use to get through to your prospects in a way that you have never before been able to use.

Here's a roundup of what you learned.

1. You have learned about the behavior of charismatic people. What makes some people so successful? You learned how people think, how your prospects relate to you, and how you can get through to them. You now know that there are three modes people fit into, namely sight-based, sound-based, and feeling-based, or visual, auditory, and kinesthetic. You found out that these various types want to be dealt with in their own particular way.

2. You learned about visuals. You heard that visuals' minds work like a photo album full of snapshots. They look up to the right, up to the left, or straight ahead in understanding you when you speak. They use words like *show, bright, clear, view,* and *see.* You found out that visuals want to see your ideas. They want you to match their predicates and talk in their language. They want you to show them a lot of illustrations and want to get understanding and comprehension more quickly by visualizing your message.

3. You learned that the minds of auditories works like a jukebox, the arm picking the record out, putting the record on a platter, and then playing the record to understand what you are talking about. These auditories want to hear your message delivered well. They get a lot out of sounds. They used words like *hear, ring, sound,* and *tell.* Like visuals, auditories want you to match their predicates and use the words that they think in. They want to listen to the inflection of your voice. They want you to use cute sayings and illustrations. They want soft background music, and they want you to verbally explain illustrations; they don't want to read them.

4. You learned about kinesthetics, or people that are feeling-based. These individuals get a good or bad impression of you very quickly. They use words like *feel, impression, grab,* and they want you to use the words they typically communicate with. These people want you to give them things they can hold. They want to become involved in the conversation. They want to experience it. They want you to get them to experience and feel the interview and presentation.

5. Next you learned some highly useful techniques for getting rapport. You learned how to use active listening in small talk as a means of generating trust and warmth. You now know how to match key words, or the words on which people put the most importance during communication. These words and phrases reflect the frame of reference or the experience level of your prospect. You learned to match these words and

phrases to get your prospects to better understand your message, and you found out how to match predicates in the visual, auditory, and kinesthetic see-hear-feel style of your product.

You gained information about voice quality—pace, pitch, timbre, tone. If you match or mirror the right way, you will create higher comfort levels in your prospect. You also learned how to mirror body movements: how to increase trust by using your hands, legs, even your posture by matching and mirroring your prospect. This causes more warmth and rapport. I also covered crossover mirroring. You learned techniques on how to break rapport in certain meetings if you want to. If there's a person you don't want to talk to, or if the meeting is going along a pathway that is uncomfortable for you, you can disrupt it without anyone knowing what you did.

6. We covered how to change your own as well as your prospect's emotions. You realized that there are very unique ways to answer visually, auditorily, and kinesthetically by doing things like raising your eyebrows for the visuals, by making sounds or noises for the auditories, or touching the kinesthetics.

You also heard about how to steal anchors or how to get your prospect to understand your concepts five times as fast by using the same symbols nonverbally that your prospects use on other people. You learned how to lift your eyebrows and nod your head at the right time. You now can take your prospect's mannerisms and use them back on him.

You heard how to get your prospect to be more open and accepting of you and how to keep him from feeling stuck in an objection by changing his thought mode to another thought mode. You know that if he's stuck on price, you can move him into another product benefit that may not be price-related. In other words, you learned how to move him from a seeing mode to a feeling or hearing mode.

You also found out about hidden commands— embedded commands that you can make in your own stories in which you use autosuggestion, or hypnosis, if you will, to get your prospect to act on your message.

You learned extremely useful steps in cashing emotions, and how to get your prospect's outcome to find out what he really wants. So all you really need to do is give it to him and to dovetail his needs and outcomes with your own.

You now know to use things like asking your prospect in the beginning of the interview what he may want from you or how you and help him. You know how to get your prospect involved in your message by using metaphors and stories that tie in loosely to his own experience or situation. You learned to get your prospect to see, feel, and hear himself in the situation of buying the product by getting him to experience it through your story or parable.

7. You gained useful techniques that can change the way you sell, and you also realized that much of this is common sense. These are things people tend to do naturally, but if you can

make them tools instead of accidents, you can sell more than you have ever been able to sell before, because you can make this common sense into common practice, and common practice into common money.

By remembering these techniques, you will possess more useful information than many other salespeople have. You will gain strength and ability to communicate with people in exactly the way they want to be communicated with. You have gained some very intricate techniques, which, however simple, will work for you. You will double or triple your business in a very short amount of time.

Recently I wrote an article for a large insurance sales magazine. One month later I got a letter back from a gentleman in central Pennsylvania who wrote me saying, "Dear Kerry, I've been using what I thought were extremely good standard sales techniques for about five years. My business was doing well but not great. Kerry, I used some of the techniques outlined in your article about the visuals, auditories, and kinesthetics, finding outcomes, anchoring, as well as instant replay. I wouldn't have thought this possible so quickly, but I have received three more sales this week alone that I don't think would have happened if I would have not used the information."

It is up to you to make these ideas useful. Don't try to apply them all at once. Use a couple of different techniques every day. Read this book at least five more times to get something out of it each time that you didn't get before. Apply this knowledge, and you will do much better than this gentleman in Pennsylvania. You will increase your business more than 50 percent, because knowledge is power, power is flexibility, and flexibility is having the options you need to do the right thing at the right time.

CPSIA information can be obtained
at www.ICGtesting.com
Printed in the USA
LVHW032158110220
646616LV00004B/5